Lessons from Laodicea

Lessons from Laodicea

Missional Leadership in a Culture of Affluence

ROSS A. LOCKHART

Foreword by Darrell L. Guder

CASCADE *Books* · Eugene, Oregon

LESSONS FROM LAODICEA
Missional Leadership in a Culture of Affluence

Cascade Books
An Imprint of Wipf and Stock Publishers
199 W. 8th Ave., Suite 3
Eugene, OR 97401

www.wipfandstock.com

PAPERBACK ISBN 13: 978-1-4982-3903-5
HARDCOVER ISBN 13: 978-1-4982-3905-9

Cataloguing-in-Publication data:

Lockhart, Ross A.

Lessons from Laodicea : Missional Leadership in a Culture of Affluence / Ross A. Lockhart.

xxvi + 166 pp. ; 23 cm. Includes bibliographical references.

ISBN: 978-1-4982-3903-5 (paperback) | ISBN: 978-1-4982-3905-9 (hardback)

1. Mission of the church—United States. 2. Mission of the church—Canada. 3. Christianity 21st century. I. Title.

BV2070 .L4 2016

Manufactured in the U.S.A.   03/28/2016

For Laura,
who reminds me daily through
marriage and ministry
that discipleship means joy.

Contents

Foreword by Darrell L. Guder | ix

Preface: Botox or Bypass? | xiii

Acknowledgments | xvii

Introduction: The Laodicean Captivity of the Church | xix

Part I: Living in Laodicea

Chapter One
Canaanite Idol—Gideon's Prime Time Debut | 3

Chapter Two
I'm Not Rich
(and Other Laodicean Lies of the 1 Percent) | 12

Chapter Three
Don't Make Baby Jesus Cry
(and Other Handy Ways to Domesticate the Gospel) | 23

Chapter Four
Here I Am to Worship
(the Unholy Trinity of Me, Myself, and I) | 34

Chapter Five
Full of It? Beyond Bankrupting Functional Atheism | 45

Part II: Leaving Laodicea Behind

Chapter Six
Fifty Shades of Grace—Lessons from Jonah
(Call, Confusion, Confession, Conversion, Community) | 55

Chapter Seven
Q3 Minority Report: Following Jesus in the Ruins of Christendom | 66

Chapter Eight
Five Mark' "S" of the New "Missional Community" | 103

Chapter Nine
Missional Microwave: Holy Spirit Lessons on Heating Up
Lukewarm Leadership | 131

Chapter Ten
Hurry on Down—the Price is Right
(Zacchaeus-Like Faith in the World Today) | 147

Conclusion: Silver and Gold I Have None—The Laodicean Cure? | 155

Bibliography | 163

Foreword

The missional theological discussion, as it has unfolded in the last years, has evidenced significant areas of consensus together with a great diversity of complementary and conflicting responses. There is, for example, a general consensus that Christendom, at least the Western Latin-based strand of it, is over or is ending. This is generally regarded as an opportunity to engage the church's ancient apostolic mission anew, and to do so by confronting the problematic compromises and reductionisms that have accompanied the linkage of church and state.

That text entails reading our Christendom legacy dialectically, recognizing in the centuries of Western Christendom many evidences of God's faithfulness interacting with human rebellion and compromise. Simplistic dismissals of the cultural and theological legacy of Western Christendom are not an option. Nor is the commitment to read and interpret this history with critical openness and to name the cultural captivities honestly and bravely an option. Our vocation requires such risk-taking honesty, especially today.

Supporting and guiding this confrontation of Christendom's captivities is the reclamation of a distinctive understanding of the authority of Scripture for the church. "Missional hermeneutics" is emerging as the disciplined engagement of the biblical text as the Spirit empowered instrument for the continuing formation of faithfully witnessing communities. Such interpretive strategies investigate how the text continued the apostolic formation of such communities then, and how it does so today. Missional hermeneutics thus takes seriously the fundamental missional vocation of every gathered community to continue the witness to Christ in a particular context.

The seven letters that open the Revelation of St. John are intriguing examples of such ongoing biblical formation of these distinctive Christian communities in Asia Minor. They reveal how intimately the Lord of the church knows these congregations of witnesses. Coupled with that intimate knowledge is the clarity of the commission he has given each one to serve him as his witnesses. They are carrying out that commission in diverse ways, reflecting obedience, struggle, confidence, and profound problems. There is a prophetic sense in which the situations of these seven churches anticipate challenges that the Christian movement will face throughout its history. We study them with gain as they guide us to recognize in our own corporate lives as witnessing congregations where and why our Lord affirms, comforts, accuses, and judges us. Empowered by the Holy Spirit, these texts can profoundly shape us today so that we can walk worthy of the calling with which we have been called (Eph 4:1).

Ross Lockhart finds in the letter to Laodicea a serious missional crisis in this first-century community that merits close attention on the part of contemporary communities emerging from Christendom, especially in North America. The crisis is exposed in the claim of that community, cited by its Lord: "For you say, I am rich, I have prospered, and I need nothing" (Rev 3:17). Their affluence, and their reliance upon it, make them subject to profound judgment: ". . .you are wretched, pitiable, poor, blind, and naked" (ibid.). The threat is that the Lord will "spew them out of [his] mouth" (Rev 3:16). Lockhart suggests that the unfaithfulness of the spiritually threatened Laodicean church is not only a problem then but a prophetic pointer toward a crisis that threatens Christianity today, especially in the cultures shaped by the Constantinian establishment. The impact of that legal and cultural establishment upon the apostolic churches from the fourth century onward was that they became affluent, owners of property and managers of wealth.

The New Testament communities founded by the apostolic missionaries were marginal, vulnerable, insecure, and unprotected communities. They were subject to persecution. Part of their formation as disciples becoming apostles was our Lord's emphasis upon the suffering that would often result from their witness. They were to take up their cross and follow Jesus. There is in the New Testament no trace of any expectation that Jesus' mission would ultimately lead to political status and cultural clout. There is no mention of a building defined as a "church" in the Bible. When establishment comes, a different kind of persecution begins to shape the church: the temptations of power, property, privilege, and protection. The letters in the Revelation of St. John, together with the synoptic accounts of Jesus' temptation in the wilderness, are astonishingly relevant examples of missional formation for the Constantinian church and its heirs.

It is that relevance which Lockhart explores in this book. He focuses upon the responsibility of the church's leadership today to equip congregations to recognize their captivity to affluence and the threat to their faithful witness which that captivity engenders. The "default mode" of Western Christendom is "institutional maintenance," which relies upon land, real estate, endowments concrete treasures where our hearts are also. That reliance upon affluence reflects, as Lockhart documents, our culture's idolization of affluence. It is not only a problem "out there" in the unchurched world. It is a reality that shapes virtually every dimension of the church's life, faith, and action. Thus, to encounter the gospel is to be confronted with a conversion from bondage to affluence to liberated service of God's kingdom. Both the biblical witness and a sober reading of our context of affluence require that the church "come to Jesus" anew in order to be equipped for our witness. The author's program spells out what it means for the late and post-Christendom church today to "not be conformed to this world, but be transformed by the renewal of your mind, that you may prove what is the will of God, what is good and acceptable and perfect" (Rom 12:2).

Darrell L. Guder
Princeton, New Jersey

Preface
Botox or Bypass?

Is there no balm in Gilead? Is there no physician there?
Why then is there no healing for the wound of my people?

—Jeremiah 8: 22

"Botox Defense Adds a New Wrinkle to the Legal Lexicon." The attention-getting headline from a local newspaper, went on to offer more juicy details of a fifty-one-year-old woman's legal defense while representing herself during a trial on a charge of refusing to give a breath sample at the roadside.[1] Apparently, the driver was pulled over by the local police shortly after midnight, driving half the posted speed limit and weaving dangerously on the highway. She was given four chances to blow into a Breathalyzer, failing to register a sample each and every time.

Her defense? The driver argued in court that she couldn't purse her lips properly around the Breathalyzer because of Botox injections she received a week earlier while on holidays in Mexico. The driver did admit to drinking alcohol the night of her arrest, but did not comment on how many drinks she consumed. It would be just as interesting to know how she could sip a glass of wine without spilling it down the front of herself after that Botox treatment! Surprisingly, the judge dismissed all charges after being presented with a letter from "Dr. Botox" in Mexico confirming the recent

1. Jane Seyd, *North Shore News,* October 22, 2010.

treatments. Lawyer friends of mine tell me it's now being referred to with amusement and bewilderment simply as "the Botox defense."

Not long after reading this story I found myself in the doctor's office for my annual check up. I noticed a large, new sign in the waiting room that read, "Effective January 1st, our clinic is pleased to offer patients regular Botox treatments for a set fee." Really? I teased my doctor, "is that what healthcare has come to—injections for big puffy lips?" My doctor smiled and said, "Hey, some people think they need that stuff. You know, nip and tuck—a little fix here, a little help there. Maybe it's the same in your business, Reverend," he said with a warm smile and a wink. Ouch.

That got me thinking. Is that how people view faith and spirituality today? A little nip and tuck on their moral character; a wee "enhancement" of their soul; a weekly "boost" or injection of faith in order to see them through the days ahead?

I love my adopted home in the Pacific Northwest. Cascadia, the region that includes Oregon, Washington state, and British Columbia, is a unique, beautiful, and soulful part of God's creation.[2] As I said to a congregation not long after arriving on the West Coast, "Some of you were born here, and the rest of us got here as fast as we could." And it's true. Heaven is a local call in the land of lattes and Lululemon. But I often wonder, after serving congregations across Canada and global church service from Africa to Northern Ireland, why do people here appear to be so resistant to active involvement in a worshipping community? I've never lived in a place like Cascadia before. You know, where everyone is comfortable with "spirituality," but freezes up, and run the other way with yoga mats, if you try and place that "spirituality" within a particular religious tradition. Spirit—yes. God—uh oh. Jesus—whoa.

In no way do I want to diminish or scoff at Cascadians' spirituality. It's a great starting place. I have a deep affection for the doctrine of prevenient grace—the notion that before we know or love God, God knows and loves us. God as covenant maker and covenant keeper—that's important. So, evangelistic conversations are different here in Cascadia. People will discuss spiritual things, but often clam up when you try and locate that spirituality within a specific tradition. If one stays in that place too long, of course, the danger is that spirituality just becomes a nice, but not necessary, addition

2. For a fulsome treatment of the unique culture and spiritual dimension of the Pacific Northwest explore journalist Doug Todd's work *Cascadia*. For a quirky look at the region (including Cascadia's own flag) lose yourself for a few minutes on the website www.cascadianow.org.

to an already perfect life. Cascadian spirituality, left on its own, may not move people to a state of justification, instead allowing them to use the "Botox defense" against the possibility of a relationship with the living God revealed in Jesus Christ, crucified and risen. Or, as Darrell Guder so aptly names the danger, "an imaginary, non-incarnational, docetic spirituality."[3] Our story as Christians—or perhaps more humbly, people who are trying to figure out what it means to follow Jesus—is not a story of Botox, but bypass.

I had a visit this past spring with a church friend who spent the weekend in hospital with chest pains. I descended the staircase at our local hospital to the emergency ward and checked in with the harried nurse. I followed the wave of her dismissive hand to the cardiac assessment unit, and there was the man resting uneasily on a narrow bed, complete with shiny railings and plastic sheets. We talked about his situation and the tests that were being run. It looked like surgery was the next step. "There's no simple fix . . . my doctor told me," the man said, looking rather grim. "This is going to require an intervention that may either give life or take it away." Now the stakes were higher. I could see it in his eyes. "Would you pray with me?" he asked quietly, his voice breaking with emotion.

I saw that look again later in the same week when people came forward in the chapel on Ash Wednesday. A hearty number of pilgrims, seeking their own balm in Gilead, filled the wee space as rain danced from the outside on stained glassed images of prophets Micah, Isaiah, and Jeremiah. As I scanned the congregation, I knew some of their stories and needs but was glad on that day that God knew the full story. As they made their way forward down the aisle, the texts of the day were still ringing in their heads and echoing in their hearts:

> "Even now," declares the Lord, "return to me with all your heart,
> with fasting and weeping and mourning."

> "Create in me a clean heart, O God, and put a new and right
> spirit within me."

> "For where your treasure is, there your heart will be also."

Last year's palm branches dissolved into a black and smelly heap of ashes. I leaned forward and accepted the Word of God's judgment on this "death-denying culture." The woman gently marked my forehead with the sign

---

3. Guder, *Continuing Conversion*, 105.

of the cross and whispered something between a fact and a promise: "Remember you are dust and to dust you shall return."

I returned to my wooden pew and sat waiting in anticipation. Waiting . . . as I did in my own doctor's office for that annual check up. Waiting . . . as I did with the church member trying to get a handle on the doctor's diagnosis. Waiting . . . as a child of God, a recovering sinner, a follower of the One whose cross is before but whose yoke is easy and burden is light. Waiting . . . knowing that the life of faith worth living is not about easy or quick fixes. Waiting . . . with a keen awareness that there is no "Botox Christianity" worth seeking nor serving in Cascadia or anywhere else. Waiting . . . on the One who the tradition calls "The Great Physician" who alone can bypass my sin and at last, "Create in me a clean heart, O God."

Acknowledgments

The Word became flesh and blood and moved into the neighborhood.
—John 1: 14, The Message.

This book first began to take shape as I strolled through the Goreme Open-Air Museum in the Cappadocia region of eastern Turkey. It was my second visit to that beautiful land and as I toured the empty cave churches, with their stunning frescos of the Christian faith painted boldly on the walls, I could not help but reflect on home and wonder about the future of the North American church navigating through the ruins of Christendom. There I was standing in a once-vibrant Christian community now turned into a cold and somber art museum. I could almost hear the whispered witness of those who once lived, prayed, laughed, ate, and loved one another as Jesus commanded them. The gaunt and fading frescos of Christ on the walls of those ancient cave churches felt like a warning to me. The sovereign God we know in Jesus Christ builds and dismantles the "church visible" according to the Spirit's mission in the world. I wondered how we might, in a North American culture of affluence, remain faithful to the risen Christ who is on the loose in our neighborhoods wherever we live, work, and play. I wondered what it might mean to be the sent people of God, living and sharing the gospel in this twenty-first-century individualistic, secular, and consumerist North American culture.

My return to Canada and subsequent writing has been full of treasured conversations and prayerful reflection. I am indebted to the academic

Acknowledgments

institutions where I am privileged to teach: St. Andrew's Hall, The Vancouver School of Theology, and St. Mark's College at The University of British Columbia. I am equally grateful for my weekly guest preaching in local churches across the country where faithful disciples teach me what God is up to in their neighborhoods. I am thankful for the opportunity to test out and receive feedback on early drafts of this work through speaking invitations at the Cruxifusion conference, St. Mark's College Lenten Lecture Series, the Presbyterian Synod of Saskatchewan, and the Epiphany Explorations conference. I am especially beholden to friends and colleagues who read drafts of this book and improved it greatly by their suggestions and encouragement, including Richard Topping, Jason Byassee, Will Willimon, Robert Fennell, Ed Bentley, and Darrell Guder. To Darrell in particular, I owe a deep and sincere thank you for writing such a thoughtful Foreword to this work.

I also wish to express my heartfelt thanks to the good folks at Cascade Books for their support and encouragement throughout the publishing process. A special word of thanks to my editor Rodney Clapp and his commitment to making this work a more faithful witness to the gospel.

Finally, it has been said that behind every successful person there stands a surprised spouse. What most pastors/professors will tell you, however, is that behind every faithful person stands an even more prayerful spouse. From coast to coast, and around the world, it has been a tremendous blessing to share life and ministry with my wife Laura. Together, we give God thanks for kingdom work, including the stewardship of raising Emily, Jack, and Sadie. To Laura be the thanks and to God be the glory!

Ross A. Lockhart,
St. Andrew's Hall, Vancouver.

Introduction
The Laodicean Captivity of the Church

What good is it for someone to gain the whole world, yet forfeit their soul?

—Mark 8: 36

"Pick up your cross and follow me," a friend winked, cheerfully teasing our group of pilgrims bubbling away in the warmth of the hot springs of Pamukkale. The delightful resort town in western Turkey has welcomed visitors down through the ages seeking its restorative properties. In fact, Pamukkale once went by another name—Hierapolis. Hierapolis was famous during Greco-Roman times as a commercial city and military colony in the Lycus Valley. Its distinctive "white castle postcard" look and warm-water baths gave it a resort feeling long before discount websites offered "weekend spa getaways." Our group was on a pilgrimage in the footsteps of Paul and as the pilgrimage leader, I made the decision to detour for a few days to explore the Seven Churches of the Revelation.

As we relaxed in the warm water, we were only about ten kilometers (six miles) north of Laodicea. Unlike touristy Pamukkale, Laodicea today sits mostly abandoned under layers of dirt. From the motor coach, if you blink you will miss it. In the days of the early church, however, Laodicea was the most important city in the Lycus River Valley, nestled between Hierapolis and Colossae and quite a distance east of Ephesus. Laodicea was on a major thoroughfare making it a banking, finance, and textile center as well as a decent spot to catch the gladiator games. It was on the "right side of the tracks" and its posh inhabitants liked to show off their wealth. When an earthquake destroyed the city in 60 AD, the locals turned down "government money" and simply paid for the rebuilding of the city out of their own pockets. Excavations have revealed such luxuries in Laodicea as a gymnasium, two theatres, a stadium, and a sophisticated water system. The "Beverly Hills" of the Roman province of Asia, Laodicea is mentioned in Paul's letters, for example Colossians 4:13–16, but is perhaps best known in John's writing as the "lukewarm" church:

> And to the angel of the church in Laodicea write: The words of the Amen, the faithful and true witness, the origin of God's creation: "I know your works; you are neither cold nor hot. I wish that you were either cold or hot. So, because you are lukewarm, and neither cold nor hot, I am about to spit you out of my mouth. For you say, "I am rich, I have prospered, and I need nothing."[1]

The imagery of hot/cold/lukewarm is fascinating. As we bubbled away in Pamukkale our group reflected on this letter to the angel of the church in Laodicea. Laodicea sat between the bubbling hot water of Hierapolis (swirling all around us) and the cool waters of Colossae. Those "lukewarm" Christians thought they had everything they ever needed to be happy, successful, and popular. But Revelation rebukes their pride, stating bluntly, "You do not realize that you are wretched, pitiable, poor, blind, and naked." These "tepid talmidim" or disappointing disciples required "gold" refined by the fires of testing and long-suffering patience. Laodicea was known for its famous medical school and it's "Phrygian powder" eye cream. So, for good measure Revelation adds that divine "eye salve" of even greater value must be applied so that they can finally see the gospel at work all around them.

Long after returning home to North America, that image of bubbling away upstream from lukewarm Laodicea in the warm waters of ancient Hierapolis remains. The "Phrygian powder" may still have some effectiveness after all these years, since a visit to Pamukkale opens one's eyes to the Laodicean captivity of the church in North America today. Events in Western culture like the Occupy movement, with its division of the world into the noble "99 percent" and Disney-like "1 percent" villains, have both raised awareness of our captivity but also enabled most middle-class North Americans to get off the hook when it comes to our participation in

1. Revelation 3:14–17, *NIV*.

systemic structures of corporate sin that repress the world's poor. Like the Jubilee movement a decade earlier, as Christians we are invited to reflect on our own role in the systems that continue to help "the rich get richer" while the poor get poorer.

As Christians, we live within a North American culture today that is built on the bedrock of materialism and consumerism. As Soong-Chan Rah argues

> Materialism and consumerism reduced people to a commodity. An individual's worth in society is based upon what assets they bring and what possessions they own. The commodification of human life means that we are more than willing to terminate human life if the cost is deemed too high, whether that is the killing of an unborn child because he or she will cause undue financial strain on society or the killing of a prisoner because it costs more to keep him incarcerated. Social life is reduced to the exchange of goods and products, and human life is reduced to a consumable value based upon material worth above and beyond any spiritual worth. Materialism also creates a sense of urgency in having our personal needs met. Because everything has a price and can be made affordable, we have been conditioned to expect quick and easy answers to problems. These answers always come in the material realm and we begin to believe that our spiritual problems can be solved with material goods. . . . The Western, white captivity of the church means that the church has wholeheartedly adapted the materialistic and consumeristic worldview of (North) American culture.[2]

Without naming it as such, Soong-Chan Rah is describing the Laodicean captivity of the church in North America. The language of the "Laodicean captivity of the church" harkens back to the Protestant Reformation and Martin Luther's classic 1520 work "On the Babylonian Captivity of the Church," likening the Mother Church's abuse and control of the sacraments to the exile period of Israel under the Babylonians. For Luther, it was a doctrinal captivity of the church showing the lack of grace and faith in Christ compared to the community revealed through the love of God: Father, Son and Holy Spirit.

Five hundred years later, in a similar way today, the mainline church's decline in Western society bears the marks of a community that has stopped living out the radical, mutual, self-giving love that is at the heart of the

---

2. Rah, *Next Evangelicalism*, 49.

Trinity. Christian worship in captivity that is focused more on performance for the sake of consumers of religion—whether that is dry ice, lasers, and praise bands, or robed choirs and *Phantom of the Opera*-spooking organs—sits in lukewarm water. Christian communities that demand little of their members but allow them to demand much of the church by meeting their "personal needs" find themselves in captivity. Christian communities that have accepted that the best way to "do church" is to allow disciples to "outsource their baptismal vows" to paid clergy swim in captivity. "I did it my way" de facto doctrine pops up in cultures of affluence that allow human beings to see God's grace as "nice but not necessary" and wrap secular humanism in liturgical garb for aesthetic pleasure alone. Captivity.

Through the movement of the Holy Spirit, however, it is exciting to "pray attention" to where Christian leaders are able to witness to where the gospel is confronting the dominant powers of this age. One such place is the ministry and writing of Pope Francis I. In one of his earliest works as Pope, the Vatican released in 2013 *Evangelii Gaudium (The Joy of the Gospel)*, where Francis states boldly, "The Gospel joy which enlivens the community of disciples is a missionary joy." Francis speaks directly to the "Laodicean captivity" of the church by stating that Christians have a fundamental choice facing us today between an "evangelizing Church that comes out of herself" and a "worldly Church that lives within herself, of herself, for herself."

Missionary outreach, Pope Francis declares, must be "paradigmatic for all the Church's activity." All Church institutions, from the papacy to parishes, must be reformed so that their structures are directed not toward maintenance, but toward a permanent state of mission.[3]

Pope Francis also summons all people to a similar process of conversion, remarking that those who are truly disciples will be missionary disciples, characterized by the joy of the faith. This notion that everyone, from pastors to elders to laypeople are called by their baptism to be missionary disciples is deep in the DNA of those of us within the Reformed tradition. It's ironic that it takes the pope of the Catholic Church to remind us of our vocation as missionary disciples in the world. So that there would be no misunderstanding, Francis makes clear what missionary disciples engaged in confronting the powers of the world and evangelizing creation should look like. Missionary disciples as evangelizers, should never look

---

3. *Evangelii Gaudium*, 25.

like "someone who has just come back from a funeral" but rather Francis encourages Christians to recover and deepen that

> delightful and comforting joy of evangelizing, even when it is in tears that we must sow. . . And may the world of our time, which is searching, sometimes with anguish, sometimes with hope, be enabled to receive the good news not from evangelizers who are dejected, discouraged, impatient or anxious, but from ministers of the Gospel whose lives glow with fervor, who have first received the joy of Christ.[4]

The church in the West today finds itself in a "Laodicean captivity." While the gospel spreads and thrives in the global south and east, the Western mainline church looks longingly back at Christendom and forward in fear. This work attempts to name the reality of the "Laodicean captivity" and also suggest steps towards missional leadership in a culture of affluence.

By *missional*, I mean that the essential vocation of the church is to be God's called and sent people in the world, trusting that rather than the church having a mission, God's mission has a church.[5] Recognizing that a hard-and-fast definition of "missional church" is elusive, it is possible to say missional leaders seek an alternative imagination for being the church in the world where God's Spirit is at work transforming us as a community through mystery, memory, and mission.[6] With a deep trust to the witness of the Triune God, missional leadership recognizes that God's being and doing are one, and since God's actions always flow from who God is as Father, Son, and Holy Spirit, so too should the church seek to unify its being and doing.[7]

By *affluence*, I am referring to the economic reality of, and cultural aspirations tied up with, our North American late-stage capitalist society that places a high value on, and demands a conversion to, consumerism and material wealth.[8] Theologically, following Jesus in a culture of North

---

4. Ibid., 10.

5. Guder, ed., *Missional Church*, 11. Rooted in a deep witness to the Triune God, Guder defines missional ecclesiology as biblical, historical, contextual, eschatological, and possible for all disciples to practice.

6. Roxburgh and Boren, *Introducing the Missional Church*, 45.

7. Sparks, Soerens, and Friesen, eds., *New Parish*, 81. As the Parish Collective argues, "Mission cannot be conceived as a project of the church, rather, the church exists within God's reconciling mission."

8. *The New York Times* has noted that Canadian middle class is now outstripping the United States middle class in its economic achievement and comfort of living. See

American affluence (either by enjoying economic prosperity or buying into the cultural assumption that everyone aspires to be affluent) presents multiple challenges. As the Parish Collective notes

> Economics functions as a mirror, where the truth about your faith is reflected back. The spreadsheet is a theological statement, reflecting any incongruence between what you say you believe and how you steward your resources. This reality can be painful. The close connection of economics to the practicing of your faith is reflected in the simple principle that Jesus communicated: "Where your treasure is, there your heart will be also . . ." To think of faith and economics primarily in terms of philanthropic giving is to fundamentally mistake what economics are and why they are so powerful. At a core level economics has to do with basic exchange, receiving and giving. This exchange is behind common word pairings such as spending and earning, investing and accruing, or borrowing and lending. The connection between your treasure and your heart is not simply about how you give; it's also about how you earn, which means there is nothing that has to do with money that doesn't have to do with your heart. Your heart is connected to your treasure.[9]

This book attempts to name the challenges and promises inherent in partnering with the Holy Spirit in order to offer missional leadership in a culture of affluence. It is about both living in and leaving Laodicea behind. In the first half of the book I explore the reality of living in Laodicea. I attempt to name and challenge some of the false gods that are present and vying for our allegiance in Western culture today. Chapter One explores the question of idolatry in our Western world through the "spiritual not religious" convictions of Gideon in the book of Judges. Our easygoing accommodation with the dominant culture, and its questionable values, is a mark of our Laodicean captivity in the church. Chapter Two explores the Laodicean lie of privileged North Americans trying to align themselves with the world's poor as exposed in the Occupy movement in 2011. A theological reading of this Laodicean lie suggests that the sin of pride lies just underneath the surface of our resistance to name and own our participation in corporate sin. Chapter Three explores the Western church's domestication of the gospel in order to make God's demands and promises "safe and unassuming,"

Ian Austen and David Leonhardt, "Life in Canada, Home of the World's Most Affluent Middle Class," April 30, 2014.

9. Sparks, Soerens, and Friesen, eds., *New Parish*, 97–98.

while secretly fueling the sin of envy. Chapter Four explores the destructive effective of unchecked individualism in the Laodicean captivity of the church. By placing personal preferences above partnering with the Spirit of God, we are always in danger of missing the divine call to move beyond our own interiority. Chapter Five challenges the church to turn away from functional atheism by naming the powerful influence of habitual greed at work in the captivity of Laodicea.

In the second half, I attempt to leave Laodicea behind by responding boldly to the call of the Holy Spirit to exercise missional leadership in the midst of a culture of affluence. This shift acknowledges that the Western church needs deliverance by our Sovereign God from Laodicea, for the sake of God's reconciling mission in the world. Chapter Six explores God's transforming power in the story of Jonah as a template for how we might respond to the divine call with hope of forming a new and redeemed community of faith. Chapter Seven examines three critical questions that disciples must engage in order to follow Jesus in the ruins of Christendom. Chapter Eight goes deeper and explores five critical marks of the new missional communities God is forming in the ruins of Christendom. Chapter Nine draws on the revival ministry of John Wesley to imagine ways in which the Holy Spirit is heating up the lukewarm Laodicean faith today for the sake of partnering with God's mission in the world. Chapter Ten turns to the curious encounter between Jesus and Zacchaeus as a bold sign of God's transformative power and release from Laodicean captivity of the church today. The conclusion brings this journey away from Laodicea into focus by sifting the apostles' bold healing and proclamation at the Beautiful Gate in the book of Acts. The church of Christ, set free from its Laodicean captivity, will be a church that is wary of the dominant values of the culture but one that finds ways to faithfully proclaim the gospel in the midst of hostility and fear. In many ways, the church of Christ set free from its Laodicean captivity will bear marks of another church that John's revelation names—Philadelphia:

> I know your deeds. See, I have placed before you an open door that no one can shut. I know that you have little strength, yet you have kept my word and have not denied my name. . . .I am coming soon. Hold on to what you have, so that no one will take your crown. The one who is victorious I will make a pillar in the temple of my God. Never again will they leave it. I will write on them the name of my God and the name of the city of my God, the new Jerusalem, which is coming down

out of heaven from my God; and I will also write on them my
new name.[10]

I do not attempt to write this work out of any presumption of objectivity or
detached thinking. I write acknowledging that in the course of my own attempts to follow Jesus I have often lost sight of the One who goes ahead like
a pillar of cloud by day and a pillar of fire at night. I too have been bedazzled
by the power, prestige, and payments promised by the Laodicean captivity
of the church. I write with my own particularity as a North American/Irish-
Canadian/Gen Xer/married man/father of three/Vancouver Canucks fan/
pastor turned professor/redeemed sinner/liberal evangelical/disciple of the
risen Christ whose promise to the Laodicean church gives me incredible
hope:

> "Listen! I am standing at the door, knocking; if you hear my
> voice and open the door, I will come in to you and eat with
> you, and you with me."[11]

My prayer is that missional leaders today might hear that same voice, respond with an evangelical, entrepreneurial, and effective heart, and in the
end help others to take steps towards faith in Jesus for a seat at that wide
and welcoming banquet table. The invitation is before us: "Let anyone who
has an ear listen to what the spirit is saying to the churches."[12]

10. Revelation 3:8, 11–12, *NIV.*

11. Revelation 3:20, *NRSV.*

12. Revelation 3:22, *NIV.*

Part I

Living in Laodicea

Whoever wants to save their life will lose it,
but whoever loses their life for me will find it.

—Matthew 16:25

No one can serve two lords. There is only one God, and that God will either be
the true one, who asks us to give things up when they become sin, or it will be
the god of money, who makes us turn our back on Christianity's God.

—Archbishop Oscar Romero, 21 January 1979

Chapter One

Canaanite Idol—Gideon's Prime Time Debut

If you board the wrong train, it is no use
running along the corridor in the other direction.

—Dietrich Bonhoeffer

It's funny how language changes over time. As a greying Gen Xer, I remember that if something was "rad" or "radical" as a kid that meant it was cool. Today, a radical is someone that Homeland Security would tackle at the border. Growing up, if someone talked about a mouse it was likely a rodent running around our family cottage at Lake of the Woods. Today, the first thing you think of is a device to help you navigate your computer. In a similar way the language of *idol* has shifted in contemporary culture. People speak of sports stars or Hollywood celebrities as "my idol." Luxury cars and mansions are "idolized" by the masses as something to be desired. In no small measure, the hit television show *American Idol* has helped shift the word *idol* from a negative to a positive connotation over the series's long run on the airwaves. I recall watching the debut season of *American Idol* in 2002 when "idol worship" swept across North America. Thousands of people lined up at convention centers across the country and auditioned in front of celebrity judges to win the right to compete on national television against other talented singers. As the season progressed, the judges offered their comments on people's ability—but the genius was found in the invitation for the television audience to phone in and vote on who should stay and who should go. To be honest, like watching car races for the crashes or hockey for the fights, I think a lot of us watched the show not only for the amazing entertainers but also for the selection process that revealed an astonishing number of folks who believed they could sing but whose voices were, in fact, reminiscent of fingernails on a chalkboard. Do these people not have any friends who love them enough to tell the truth? It's a little bit like that old expression that the truest measure of a man is found somewhere between the opinion of his mother and the opinion of his mother-in-law. Except in this case, it was the opinion of these contestants' families and the harsh panel of judges.

I recall an episode of *American Idol* several seasons ago where the last contestant of the evening was named Renaldo. He came out for his audition dressed head to toe in an angel costume, complete with wings and a halo. The judges were harsh, as you can imagine, especially when the only thing angelic about Renaldo was his costume and certainly not his voice. What an odd assortment of characters, I thought, as I sat on my couch watching judges, angels, and idols pass before my very eyes.

Well, this very same curious cast of characters—judges, angels, and idols—also appear before our eyes as we read the story of Gideon in the book of Judges. In fact, we owe *American Idol* a small debt of gratitude for placing the word *idol* back in our everyday vocabulary. Being more familiar with the word *idol* helps us get into some of the Old or First Testament readings a little bit easier. While our contemporary society has transformed the word *idol* into a positive concept, when we look at the word through a biblical lens there is no such translation possible. Turning to the Bible's witness in the book of Judges, we find a competition that involves idols but with stakes much higher—not *American Idol* or its poor cousin spin-off *Canadian Idol* but *Canaanite Idol*, starring Gideon and friends.

The book of Judges in general, and the character of Gideon in particular, are not parts of the Bible that most folks venture into. I often wonder if there is something inside us that feels the further and further we go back into the First Testament the harder it is to relate to our times. Yet, the character of Gideon defies this belief by presenting a lifestyle and mind-set that is remarkably contemporary.

A good way to sum up Gideon's beliefs would be to say he was "spiritual but not religious." Gideon grew up hearing stories from his parents and grandparents about God. He heard stories about how God had rescued his ancestors from slavery in Egypt, parted the Red Sea, and guided them under Moses's leadership to the promised land and so forth. But during Gideon's lifetime the people of Israel had fallen on hard times. They were oppressed by the Midianites—a foreign power—and for as much as the old folks might talk about God, Gideon had not experienced him and wondered, if their God was so great, why were their lives so miserable?

As a result Gideon and his friends had no clear allegiance to the God of Israel and were happy to kind of "mix and match" their belief systems with whatever else came along. In fact, if you were to drop by and visit Gideon and his buddies you would see them relaxing in their front yard on a Saturday afternoon grumbling about the latest raid by the Midianites, drinking a two-four of "Promised Land Pilsner" and admiring the latest idols erected in Gideon's front yard—the Asherah Pole and an altar to Baal.

While toiling away on my doctoral work, I learned a great deal about Canaanite gods and goddess as a frequent visitor to the Oriental Institute at the University of Chicago. When one enters the museum, there are seven galleries dedicated to different ancient cultures in the Middle East. Archaeologists from the University of Chicago visited the Middle East, at the time known as the Orient, back in the days when you could more easily put artifacts in your pocket "Indiana Jones style" and bring them back to Western museums. The Canaanite exhibit is exquisite. It explains how the Canaanites had many gods but El was the main creator god. His wife, the goddess Asherah, was worshipped by many throughout the region, including where the Israelites lived, by dedicating a tree that over time was often sculpted into ornate wooden poles with carvings of various shapes and designs. The image of these trees reminded me of preaching one summer in rural Connecticut where locals painted large roadside rocks like eagles, sharks, and even a huge American flag. El and goddess Asherah had a son who was known as the Canaanite god Baal. The Oriental Institute has a statue of Baal, perhaps something like what Gideon put up in his backyard. Baal was a fierce-looking warrior who was often seen holding a massive lighting bolt that gave tribute to his role as the storm god. In fact, Gideon's choice to have both an altar to Baal and an Asherah pole was a powerful combination—mixing the divine forces of storms and fertility—it's like the rainmaker meets Viagra! Of course, in a land dependent upon rain-fed agriculture and children to help work the farm you can understand why these two gods were so revered.

Gideon, feeling that the stories he learned about God from his parents and grandparents in Sunday/synagogue school were a little lame, decided to cover all his bases by mixing and matching various religious beliefs from the local area. As a result, his "spiritual but not religious" belief system was fairly shallow and totally subjective. Gideon's freedom to mix and match religious traditions is, in many ways, the most contemporary expression of a la carte spirituality available in our society today. You know, folks who feel spiritual but not religious. They express a sincere yet shallow belief system that enables them to mix and match various world religions while not belonging to any faith community. Where I live, in the Pacific Northwest, this is especially true with Eastern religions. Just recently I was chatting with a guy on the treadmill beside me at the local gym. I knew him well enough to say "Hello" from time to time but not much more than that. As we were jogging along on our adult hamster wheels he said to me, "I heard from someone that you're a pastor or something, is that right?" "Yup," I replied, debating whether telling him I was a Presbyterian would clarify or clutter the conversation. Instead I said, "How about you—are you a spiritual person?" "Oh yes," he said wiping his glowing forehead with a towel, "I'm a Buddhist." "That's great," I replied innocently, "what is it that you find compelling about the teachings of the Buddha?" Silence. He slowed his treadmill down and looked over at me like I was a space alien. "Oh, I don't know anything about that—I just like to do yoga a couple times a week." Perfect.

Subscribing to a vague notion of Eastern religion appears to be socially acceptable these days. In fact, the premier of British Columbia, Christy Clark, even tried to spend $150,000 of public money recently to shut down a major artery in our city for yoga on the Burrard Bridge. As Premier Clark said, "India has given the world a great gift in yoga, with dedicated followers around the world." She continued enthusiastically, "It's become part of the cultural fabric in B.C., and particularly so in the Lower Mainland. That's why we're inviting beginners and yogi masters alike from across the province to Vancouver—to come together to celebrate yoga in record numbers, and most importantly, have fun."[1] Where once a major North American

---

1. Brian Morton, "Premier invites yogis to Vancouver for International Day of Yoga," *Vancouver Sun*, June 5, 2015.

city might be shut down for a Billy Graham revival, today people grab their yoga mats and lattes, ready to bend bodies in a downward dog.

Now don't get me wrong. I'm not one of those folks who get all upset about yoga. It's fine as a workout and if one is actually a dedicated follower of Hinduism then expressing one's spiritual beliefs through yoga is understandable. I even have a Christian pastor friend who started her own "Yoga Chapel."[2] For years I have been involved in a multi-faith dialogue and one thing I've discovered is that all the major faith leaders I talk to see the blending of religious tradition as a worrisome trend. This "silly syncretism" is a challenge to all people of faith today. Instead of honoring the diversity of faith beliefs it tries to blend them all together like a religious Esperanto.

Now I can understand that people get turned off the church due to all sorts of reasons, many of them quite legitimate. The trouble with trying to mix and match and create your own religion is that is not connected to the living God. It is far from being rooted in community and offers no outside power to help transform your life. In fact, Gideon's "spiritual but not religious" belief system reminds me a lot of one of my favorite restaurants when I lived in Toronto.

When my wife and I were "young people in love," before children rapidly aged us and depleted us of energy and financial freedom, we used to eat out a lot living in downtown Toronto. One of our favorite spots was called Le Marche. There are many versions of this "market style" restaurant so perhaps you've had a similar experience somewhere else. When you first arrived at Le Marche you were handed a card that turned into your bill at the end of the meal. Once inside the restaurant, you had a seemingly endless variety of foods to choose from. In a crowded market atmosphere, complete with cobblestone paths and colorful umbrellas there was every possible food being prepared—offering the feeling of the United Nations taking a cooking class. You could pick up a little sushi in the seafood area, a steak and potato in another area, a tasty pizza or fresh pasta in yet another area, and on and on. And of course, there were also a section of desserts to die for, with cappuccinos and lattes to finish off your experience. Instead of paying for your meal item by item, you simply handed over the card every time you selected something and the employees stamped it with a symbol of the food or drink you were enjoying. By the end of the evening your card had a rainbow of shapes and colored stamps, and you reached the cashier

2. Rev. Bethel Lee combines Christian doctrine with the physical practice of yoga online with her ministry www.yogachapel.com.

trusting that you had made your own meal. No one else had the exact same combination as you—a unique tailor-made dining experience.

Therefore, one mark of the "Laodicean captivity" today is the general acceptance of a dominant culture force we could call "Le Marche spirituality." Pop culture encourages us to pick and choose from a whole variety of spiritual beliefs—to stamp ourselves with a little Eastern religion, a sampling of Judaism, a taste of Islam, a slice of Christianity, and a side order of New Age. What's old is new again and we live in a world drunk on this confused cocktail of a little bit of a Baal altar mixed with an Asherah fertility pole.

But as Gideon discovered, God, as covenant maker and covenant keeper, is not impressed by such an individualistic, shallow, and subjective belief system that leaves no room for the living God, and resists being rooted in a faith community and being open to the transforming power of God's grace. In fact, the Bible simply names it idolatry. Darrell Guder reminds us that at the root of idolatry is the sin that comes from the fall of humanity. Guder writes, "One can interpret the biblical teaching about human sin as the constant attempt to bring under human control what we are not qualified to control. Its most radical form, of course, is the attempt to bring God under human control."[3] This temptation for us as human creatures to control the Divine is most certainly visible in the worship of idols. One is reminded of John Calvin's warning drilled into us in the Reformed tradition that human nature is a perpetual factory of idols. As Guder argues, "The nature of sin as control is documented throughout Scripture. Idolatry is such a mechanism of control, as it reduces the divine to the level of a product of human craft and ingenuity."[4] Surely, this is not the only way to live as a person of faith in the world? If Gideon had been listening a little more carefully as a child to those old timers in the camp talking about Yahweh he might have heard (pre-Charlton Heston!) the clear command against idolatry from the Exodus experience:

> I am the Lord your God, who brought you out of Egypt, out of the
> land of slavery. You shall have no other gods before me. You shall
> not make for yourself an image in the form of anything in heaven
> above or on the earth beneath or in the waters below. You shall not
> bow down to them or worship them; for I, the Lord your God, am
> a jealous God, punishing the children for the sin of the parents to

3. Guder, *Continuing Conversion*, 76.
4. Ibid.

the third and fourth generation of those who hate me, but showing love to a thousand generations of those who love me and keep my commandments.[5]

As Gideon was about to find out, there was more to those childhood stories of God then he ever could have imagined.

One Saturday afternoon Gideon was cleaning up after his party, sweeping up the bits of Twelve Tribes Taco Chips and collecting the Promised Land Pilsner empties, when there was a loud knock at the door. Gideon opened it and saw a large angel sitting under a tree in his front yard waving him over. Gideon thought this guy was a little early for a Halloween costume party but as he got closer Gideon realized it was the real deal. The angel greeted Gideon by saying, "The Lord is with you, mighty warrior." At the moment Gideon felt anything but a mighty warrior, but as the angel continued speaking all of Gideon's skepticism and doubts diminished. Not only had he experienced an encounter with God, but he also discovered that God had a meaning and a purpose for his life. He was called to be the liberator for the people of Israel. Of course, at first Gideon had protested that surely God could find someone stronger, better connected from a powerful family. But no, God often works in mysterious and surprising ways and this was his plan for Gideon's life.

This encounter with, and experience of, the living God who Gideon had only heard about in the past through his parents and grandparents transformed his life and made him realize that the Ten Commandments were true—God *would* allow himself to be worshipped and no other gods. In fact, Gideon's mission to liberate the people of Israel begins with a Canaanite idol-smashing festival.

And what are we to make of this sudden reversal in Gideon's life story? Is this a word of hope for all those who struggle with faith just like Gideon did? Absolutely. This Bible story reminds us that God is at work in our world, not only wanting us to hear his story but encounter God and discover that God has a meaning and a purpose for us as human creatures, and the whole created order.

The Bible teaches us that the sovereign God chooses to be revealed in the world. God wants to know and to be known by human creatures. And just as God exists in loving community as Father, Son, and Holy Spirit, God invites us to join a faith community where we can experience and share the

---

5. Exodus 20:1–6, *NIV*.

love of God. As Patrick Johnson notes in relation to Karl Barth's *Church Dogmatics,*

> the community does not have the power to effect belief nor pro-
> duce knowledge of the gospel. Yet it does have the power, with all
> the human skill it can muster, to summon people to make ready
> for knowledge, and in this sense it has the responsibility to make
> a loud evangelical appeal to the world. Barth writes, "Even with
> the most powerful and heartfelt appeal which (the community)
> may make to them, it cannot change men. But with its appeal it
> can set before them the act of the love of God in which He has
> already changed them. It can make them aware that the revelation
> and knowledge of this act are awaiting them. It can thus make an
> impact in their lives and in world-occurrence . . . (and excite) a
> readiness which as such implies a small and provisional but real
> change in their being and action."[6]

Gideon learned first hand that "even with the most powerful and heartfelt appeal" he was, at first, unable to change his neighbors. Gideon follows God's command, yet it leads to conflict. In the morning when people wake up and see Gideon's altars to Baal and the Asherah pole destroyed they get angry. I wonder why? It was after all just the family altar. It's not like Gideon went out and smashed other people's idols. I believe when we experience God's grace in our lives it changes our views, our choices, and even our lifestyle, and that can be threatening to people.

I remember hearing Kathleen Norris speak at our college where she named the reality of idolatry in our contemporary lives. The author of such contemporary classics as *The Cloistered Walk* and *Amazing Grace* argued that humanity's condition is that we appear to be "natural born idolaters" since idolatry often begins innocently enough with an affection for something or someone, that eventually traps us in worship and adoration that edges God out of our devotional life. Norris argued that idolatry appears early on in the Ten Commandments because to break the other commandments you first have to go through the idolatrous action of replacing worship of God with something or someone else.[7]

As Gideon discovered, smashing the idols in our lives will expose us to the anger and scorn of those around us who cling consciously or

6. Johnson, *Mission of Preaching*, 94. Johnson is quoting Barth in *Church Dogmatics* IV/3.2

7. Norris, "What the Desert Has to Teach Us," public lecture, Vancouver School of Theology, June 12, 2015.

unconsciously to the idols that control their lives. Michael Frost reminds us that "the Western church seems to be in cultural captivity" to capitalism's idolizing of money and wealth. Quoting Michael Schluter, Frost notes that a whole culture obsessed with capital lends itself "to the idolatry of wealth at a personal level, and the idolatry of economic growth at a corporate and national level."[8] Walter Brueggemann takes the argument further, stating, "the central conflict with the gospel in our time has to do with socio-economic, political practices which bespeak theological idolatry, an idolatry which has come to exercise sovereignty over most of our life."[9]

I believe that Gideon shows us both the joy and the price for a life of faith with God. Gideon is finally free when he removes the idols, those things demanding his loyalty that stand between him and God. Living in the reality of our "Laodicean captivity," what might be standing between you and a relationship with God today? What might you have to take down, move aside, and sweep away in order to bask in the brilliant light of the resurrection morn? For some it may be an addiction to alcohol, drugs, pornography, or who knows what else . . . for others it may be the insatiable North American appetite for new things—cars, homes, jewelry—and for others it may be their self-image: their need to control their appearance, their contacts, their reputations. What idol is demanding your loyalty today?

The good news is that Gideon didn't think he was up to the challenge. The competition of Canaanite idolatry seemed too fierce for him to win. Public opinion turned against him but little did he know that he would win the Canaanite idol contest and go on to become a more famous judge than Simon Cowell, Randy Jackson, or Paula Abdul. Gideon accomplished these things not by his own power but by the power of God working through him and others. Whatever the idol is in your life today—standing between you and your relationship with God—God can and will give you the power to overcome it. All you have to do is ask. Missional leadership in a culture of affluence trusts that by God's grace and through Christ's power

Idols are deformed
Relationships transformed
The church reformed
Justice performed
Hearts strangely warmed.

8. Frost, *Road to Missional*, 73.

9. Brueggemann, *Biblical Perspectives on Evangelism*, 40.

Chapter Two

I'm Not Rich
(and Other Laodicean Lies of the 1 Percent)

Give us, Lord God, a vision of our world as your love would make it:
where the weak are protected, and none go hungry or poor;
where peace is built with justice, and justice is guided by love; and give us the
inspiration and courage to build it, through Jesus Christ our Lord.

—Corrymeela Community, Northern Ireland

The summer of 2009 my family arrived in our hometown of Markethill, Northern Ireland to serve the little Presbyterian church where my grandfather "raised the music" and where my kinfolk still take up a quarter of the pews. Stepping off the airplane in the Dublin airport, we found the local newspaper headlines already calling the last few months the beginning of the "Great(er) Depression." It had been two years since I had last been back to visit family in Ireland and the evidence of rapid economic decline was everywhere. It wasn't exactly an *Angela's Ashes* kind of moment, but after a decade of significant economic growth the Celtic tiger was looking caged and fearful in a third-rate circus train.

I'm Not Rich

Three months later, when we returned to North America, the economic reality on the ground there looked just as bleak. From 2008 to 2009 we learned that banks apparently were *not* "too big to fail." Subprime mortgages were *not* the homeowner's dream they promised to be. Massive job losses combined with bleak prospects for economic recovery shook our confidence in "human progress," akin to the pre-World War I generation so aptly described by Barbara Tuchman in *The Proud Tower*. Gen Xers and millennials realized that their adult lives might not look as posh and comfortable as those of the baby boomers that came before them. Heavy debt, discouraging employment prospects, and a growing gap between rich and poor at the expense of the middle class raised social conscience in a whole new way.

Two years later, in 2011, while economic troubles continued to plague the global economy, a group of protestors gathered in Zuccotti Park in Manhattan to launch the Occupy Wall Street movement. Leveraging the power of social media so evident in the Arab Spring of 2011, the Occupy movement spread around the world in a variety of expressions that highlighted the growing economic disparity between rich and poor, with a focus on the culpability of corporations and government in enhancing the gap, year after year. While trying to get the various Occupy movements on the same page felt like trying to herd kittens, overall there was a sense that this global justice movement attempted to reverse the growing hierarchy of wealth, and name the power and influence of corporations over governments' and countries' economic development as a worrisome threat to democracy in a globalized economy.

Globalization itself has long been studied and critiqued by scholars in all fields, including theology. Richard Bauckham summarizes the challenge as he wrestles with Christian witness in a postmodern world:

> Globalization describes the way the world is rapidly becoming a whole in which the parts interact and relate to each other, almost independently of geography. The modern media and the new information technology have much to do with this. But more specifically the phenomenon we are addressing is economic globalization or the dominance of global capitalism. This is undoubtedly a western-dominated process in which a purportedly universal ideology—unfettered free-market capitalism as a self-evident good—serves the economic interests of those with economic power. Globalization is the new imperialism, a purely economic rather than political imperialism. Globalization has

succeeded the older idea of progress in that it reduces progress to economic growth, which is supposed to bring all other goods in its train. Globalization tells a story—and its success has a lot to do with the convincingness of this story—about the irresist-ible triumph of global capitalism, about the universalizing of the culture it promotes.[1]

The Occupy movement, from its very beginning, was a push back against the enormous influence of globalization upon our culture and values in the early twenty-first century.

For as dramatic as the images were coming out of Zuccotti Park in New York City in 2011, the world's attention shifted to a growing group of protestors in London. Barred by police action from protesting in the finan-cial district, the Occupy community there moved to the front steps of the iconic St. Paul's Cathedral. Welcomed at first by church officials, the ongo-ing presence of protesters and overnight campers led to significant tension. Canon Chancellor Giles Fraser took the side of the protesters and resigned when the cathedral eventually turned to legal action to have the protesters removed. Steve Waters brought the "behind-the-scenes" decision-making regarding the protests at St. Paul's Cathedral in a new play entitled *Temple*. Reflecting on the impact of the Occupy movement on the steps of St. Paul's Cathedral, Giles wrote in the *Guardian*:

> It could be argued that Occupy's expression in London had a far greater effect on the church than it did on the City. Within a year of the protesters having been forcibly evicted from the steps of St Paul's in February 2012, the Anglican Communion had appointed a new Archbishop of Canterbury specifically chosen to speak mor-al purpose to bankers. Indeed Justin Welby, a former oil executive once blamed me for his becoming archbishop. In an interview I conducted with him, in the summer between the eviction and his appointment, he made his position on the protests perfectly clear: "Occupy reflects a deep-seated sense that there is something wrong, and we need to think very hard about what's wrong." Did that mean, I asked, he thought Occupy were right? "Of course they were right. Absolutely. And everything we are hearing now says that." After the whole St Paul's debacle, that needed to be said. Though I find it uncomfortable—painful even—to have these events revisited, there is an issue here that extends far beyond the

---

1. Bauckham, *Bible and Mission*, 6. Bauckham quotes Anthony Giddens from the London School of Economics as saying point blank that "globalization is the way we now live."

personalities involved. Perhaps that's why it makes a good subject for a play. The St Paul's/Occupy thing was not just a little bit of local difficulty. What was at stake, for all involved, was a theological question that takes us back to the very foundations of the Christian faith.[2]

The theological aspects of the Occupy movement are critical, as named by Fraser in his reflections on what took place at St. Paul's in the autumn of 2011. In the article Fraser asserts that St Paul's Cathedral, "designed by a scientist, speaks vividly of the cosmological God, the omnipotent God of the stars and the heavens. But it finds it much harder to speak convincingly of the poor, incarnate, vulnerable God of Bethlehem."[3] For Fraser, the God revealed in the cradle of Christ in Bethlehem was more closely aligned with the camp itself. The struggle to balance what theologians call the "economic and imminent" aspects of God as Trinity was clearly part of Fraser's dilemma as a cathedral official. He wrote, "One might say that the internal dynamics and tensions within the cathedral were those of the Trinity itself, each an articulation of the same God but pulling in different directions, one towards the eternal, another towards the temporal. . . . This is a tension inherent within the Christian faith itself."[4]

That the Occupy movement, on the steps of one of Christianity's best-known churches, might be revisited through the sanctified imagination of a playwright in a work entitled *Temple* seemed appropriate in my mind. The whole debate over our role in the world in systems of economic/systemic sin is ever present to each human generation. The language of "temple" reminded me of the classic depiction of two people who come to the temple in Jerusalem to pray:

> He told his next story to some who were complacently pleased with themselves over their moral performance and looked down their noses at the common people: "Two men went up to the Temple to pray, one a Pharisee, the other a tax man. The Pharisee posed and prayed like this: 'Oh, God, I thank you that I am not like other people—robbers, crooks, adulterers, or, heaven forbid, like this tax man. I fast twice a week and tithe on all my income.' Meanwhile the tax man, slumped in the shadows, his face in his hands, not daring to look up, said, 'God, give mercy. Forgive me,

2. Giles Fraser, "My hopes for the Occupy St Paul's drama that puts me on the stage," *The Guardian* May 24, 2015.

3. Ibid.

4. Ibid.

a sinner.'" Jesus commented, "This tax man, not the other, went home made right with God. If you walk around with your nose in the air, you're going to end up flat on your face, but if you're content to be simply yourself, you will become more than yourself."[5]

As I studied the church's reaction to the Occupy movement I found it interesting how quickly privileged middle- (to upper-) class suburban Christians felt the freedom to align themselves with the oppressed 99 percent against the wealthy elite known as the 1 percent. True, the 99 percent had a just and righteous cause to name before the powers and principalities of this world. Commenting on a report that supported the claims of the rallying cry of the 99 percent the *Economist* magazine wrote:

> Whatever the cause, the data are powerful because they tend to support two prejudices. First, that a system that works well for the very richest has delivered returns on labor that are disappointing for everyone else. Second, that the people at the top have made out like bandits over the past few decades, and that now everyone else must pick up the bill. Of course it is a little more complicated than that. But this downturn ought to test the normally warm feelings in America of the 99 percent towards the 1 percent.[6]

The struggle comes in the finger-pointing at the 1 percent from those in many North American churches that have more in common *globally* with the 1 percent then they do with the poverty-stricken masses who *truly* make up the 99 percent. A former child soldier in South Sudan or a garment worker in Bangladesh appears to have more of a claim to the title "99 percent" than a suburban, white-picket fence Christian living in North American privilege. Having served as a pastor in one of the most affluent communities in Canada, I was always amazed visiting people in their multimillion dollar homes who would say to me with a straight face, "Well, I'm not rich. Not compared to (fill in the blank)." This Pharisee-like dodging of privilege in order to point the finger at others is not confined to the tony mansions of affluent suburbia. No. It trickles down throughout North America wherever there is ability to put food on the table and money to pay the bills. Carey Nieuwhof picked up on this when commenting on an article entitled, "The Shrinking American Middle Class" from the January 26, 2015 *New York Times*. The *Times* reporter looked at suburban demographics and detected a trend that the middle class is shrinking. It's shrinking, in

5. Luke 18: 9–14, *The Message.*

6. *Economist Online*, October 26, 2011.

part, because more and more of the middle class are becoming upper class. As Carey Nieuwhof observed:

> Both US and Canadian personal disposable incomes are at all time highs. There are simply more affluent people than there were decades ago, which may in part explain why so many "average" people indulge their obsessions with granite counter tops, designer homes and decent cars, even without being mega-wealthy. Naturally, this leaves a huge theological void about ministry to and with the poor, but it helps explain what's actually happening in the suburbs and increasingly with the re-urbanization of many cities as the affluent move back downtown. . . . People with money have options. Technology options. Travel options. Options for their kids. And, arguably, that affluence may be one of the factors moving them further away from a committed engagement to the mission of the local church.[7]

Darrell Guder, retired from Princeton Seminary and now my colleague as the Senior Fellow of the Centre for Missional Leadership at St. Andrew's Hall, Vancouver, told me a story of a doctoral student he supervised from a Pacific Island nation. The student made an appointment and Darrell assumed that their conversation would be about some academic struggle the student faced. Instead, the student named his theological/discipleship dilemma. The student said that growing up on his home island the family was very poor and there were countless times when the cupboard was bare. His mother would lead the family in prayer asking God to provide. Somehow, like manna from heaven, at some point in the day resources would appear—a neighbor might come over with extra food, a stranger might give them money, or some other divine interaction would occur. The student confessed that his faith and reliance on God was weakening the longer he stayed in North America. He said, "Dr. Guder, I've been here three years now and I no longer worry about where my next meal is going to come from."

To be clear, in no way am I suggesting there is some kind of inherent nobility in poverty. Not at all. Instead, I'm naming the reality that for a shocking number of God's children in the world today to be part of the *true* "99 percent" means living marginally and having no reserves to fall back on. For privileged, educated, healthy North Americans to align themselves so easily with the global "99 percent" seems naïve at best and a Laodicean

7. See http://careynieuwhof.com/2015/02/10-reasons-even-committed-church-attenders-attending-less-often/.

lie at worse. Rather than pointing a finger at others we should hear Jesus speaking directly to our affluence in Luke 6, "But woe to you who are rich, for you have already received your comfort. Woe to you who are well fed now, for you will go hungry."[8]

Perhaps it is time to look again at the parable that Jesus shared with his disciples in the temple in Jerusalem. If humanity tends to vacillate between the sins of pride and sloth, I wonder what might really be going on in the mind of the Pharisee. The parable begins with Jesus saying, "two men went up to the temple to pray." The ancient city of David was well below the temple mount and the stairs that lead to it are still there today. The stairs were alternately built, one narrow, one wide, in order to prevent people running up the steps into a holy place. To this day when you visit Jerusalem you can walk reverently up the stairs, shaped so long ago to enforce careful, slow movement towards the holiest of holies. Worshippers would sing the psalms of ascent, like Psalm 122, as they climbed these stairs.

> I rejoiced with those who said to me, "Let us go to the house of the Lord." Our feet are standing in your gates, Jerusalem. Jerusalem is built like a city that is closely compacted together. That is where the tribes go up—the tribes of the Lord—to praise the name of the Lord according to the statute given to Israel.

At the southwestern wall there was a place to pause and change your money into the official temple currency in order to make a sacrifice or buy a falafel sandwich. Next to the money changers, the ritual baths provided worshippers with a stone divider down the middle so that the unclean and clean would not touch. A man stood on a balcony and called out on the busy street "clean in the middle, unclean to the sides" as the worshippers made their way around the front and headed for the main entrance on the southern wall. The entrance, still visible today, is made up of three arches and you can picture where pilgrims would have streamed into the temple. The tax collector in the parable would have fictitiously passed through here and certainly Jesus and his disciples would have entered through this main entrance as well. There were other entrances to the temple, however, including the Robinson Arch (named after the archaeologist who discovered it). The Robinson Arch was a separate entrance that served as a kind of "first class," express entry. It was an entrance for the wealthy and some of the religious leaders who would have their ritual bath at home so as to not mingle with

---

8. Luke 6: 24–25, *NIV.*

the poor and the peasants. Perhaps this was the entrance that the Pharisee entered that day. The Bible tells us that not only did these two men both go up to the temple but also they both went to pray. To state the obvious, their prayers were totally different. The Pharisee stands to pray out loud, which was his custom, and the prayer begins all right, "God I thank you . . ." But it goes downhill from there. "God I thank you that I am not like these other people" and then he starts naming the sins (or perceived sins) of other people. Now perhaps all of us have wanted to do just that in our local church upon occasion—to stand up and say what is on our minds!

Have you ever been called out in church? I remember as a teenager visiting my family in Northern Ireland and going out on a Saturday night with my cousins for a little fun. The next morning in church, after we had all had a night of good *craic*, the minister started his sermon on the evils of drinking. He said that he was very disappointed when he parked his car the previous night in front of the pub and watched too many of the local boys going in for a pint. He then proceeded homiletically to call out the young people present in church who he saw going into the pub. I looked at my cousin Gareth and we started to slump a bit lower in the pew. "Good thing we went one town over the night before for our outing," he whispered as the sermon continued. Not a good feeling.

I wonder if that is how the tax collector felt as the Pharisee both publically shamed him and in the process managed to highlight, with great pride, his own clergy "faithfulness." The Pharisee calls out the tax collector. Not a chief tax collector but just a tax collector. A *chief* tax collector in that day—like Zacchaeus in Luke 10 (the wee little man up a Jericho sycamore tree)—was an exploitive, wealthy businessperson who bid on a particular region. The Roman Empire would set a fee for that area, the chief tax collector would pay the tax for that region in full to the Romans, and then it was his job to get the money back from the people (as well as a good deal more in a generous "commission") by employing tax collectors to go door to door. This was the type of guy in the temple that day, a hired thug who intimidated the local people on behalf of a wealthy businessman and who would be despised by locals for supporting the occupying Roman army and administration. And yet, it is this man, this tax collector, who Jesus singles out for praise. It is this man who does not stand and boast with vain pride about his goodness but who lies down and begs for mercy from God. It is this man, not the other, who went home justified, which is old churchy language for "made right" with God.

Well, what do we make of this story? What does this have to do with the righteous 99 percent stand against the evil 1 percent in our day? It has a lot to do with pride. The sin of pride is a tricky issue. After all, do we not try and instill in our children and grandchildren a sense of pride? Do we not tell people in school or on the soccer pitch "well done" for scoring that goal or that A+? Is it wrong to have pride in our ourselves, our loved ones, our church, our community, and our country?

From classic theologians like Augustine to twentieth-century theologians like Karl Barth, the Christian tradition has long labeled pride as the chief sin, the source of all other sins. Why? Why pride above all other sins? Many have argued that once pride takes hold completely in the heart we fool ourselves into thinking that we have no need of God—we are self-made women and men. "What is pride," Augustine asks, "other than undue exaltation?" Or to flip the famous line attributed to C. S. Lewis on humility we could say, "Pride is not thinking too much of yourself; it is thinking of yourself too much."

When it comes to pride we often quote Proverbs 16, "Pride comes before the fall" and yet, Paul's writing in the New Testament mentions pride in a very positive sense (Rom 11:13). Is there not some way, therefore, for us to be both faithful and proud? St. Thomas Aquinas calls pride a human being's "disordered desire to be exalted that can only be corrected through the practice of humility." This parable highlights an example of both pride run amuck as well as humility. Jesus does say that those who exalt themselves will be humbled and those who are humble will be exalted. Jesus also said,

> Why do you look at the speck of sawdust in your brother's eye and pay no attention to the plank in your own eye? How can you say to your brother, "Let me take the speck out of your eye," when all the time there is a plank in your own eye? You hypocrite, first take the plank out of your own eye, and then you will see clearly to remove the speck from your brother's eye.[9]

The rush of so many privileged North Americans, with all the necessities of life so easily provided, to align themselves with the "99 percent" in judgment against the (insert maniacal laugh here) evil "1 percent" can all too easily be a prideful Laodicean lie. As C. S. Lewis warned, "How is it that people who are quite obviously eaten up with pride can say they believe in

---

9. Matthew 7:3–5, *NIV*.

God and appear to themselves very religious? I am afraid it means they are worshipping an imaginary God."[10]

No, instead we must not "off-load" our privilege and pretend to be exempt from the responsibility of our Western affluence. We must "own" it. We *should* side with the "99 percent" and recognize what liberation theologians like Gustavo Gutierrez taught us about the Bible's "preferential option for the poor." Gutierrez writes,

> the ultimate reason for commitment to the poor and oppressed is not to be found in the social analysis we use, or in human compassion, or in any direct experience we ourselves may have of poverty. These are all doubtless valid motives that play an important part in our commitment. As Christians, however, our commitment is grounded, in the final analysis, in the God of our faith. It is a theocentric, prophetic option that has its roots in the unmerited love of God and is demanded by this love.[11]

Therefore, we must acknowledge that on the sliding scale of affluence we sit much closer to the "1 percent" of the world's wealth and that our own pride often prevents us from acknowledging this truth. As Pope Francis said so well in *Evangelii Gaudium:*

> The great danger in today's world, pervaded as it is by consumerism, is the desolation and anguish born of a complacent yet covetous heart, the feverish pursuit of frivolous pleasures, and a blunted conscience. Whenever our interior life becomes caught up in its own interests and concerns, there is no longer room for others, no place for the poor. God's voice is no longer heard, the quiet joy of his love is no longer felt, and the desire to do good fades. This is a very real danger for believers too. Many fall prey to it, and end up resentful, angry and listless. That is no way to live a dignified and fulfilled life; it is not God's will for us, nor is it the life in the Spirit which has its source in the heart of the risen Christ.[12]

Like the Pharisee at the beginning of the prayer, we look up to God with what Martin Luther coined in his commentary on the Galatians as "Holy Pride." We get into all kinds of trouble, however, when we look down with judgment on others and give ourselves a "free pass" to avoid the judgment that is staring us back in the mirror.

10. Lewis, *Mere Christianity,* 104–5 (Harper Collins ed.).
11. Gutierrez, *Theology of Liberation,* xxvii.
12. *Evangelii Gaudium,* 1.2.

Part I: Living in Laodicea

Blessed
   Forgiven
      Responsible.

Chapter Three

Don't Make Baby Jesus Cry
(and Other Handy Ways to Domesticate the Gospel)

"It is easier for a camel to go through the eye of a needle than for
someone who is rich to enter the kingdom of God."

—Mark 10: 25

Today, it is all too easy to find Christians in North America decrying "secularism."[1] Secularism, that philosophical and political ideology that strives to remove religious symbols, beliefs, and influence from public life, has indeed permeated North American culture, seeing that all the world religions have an equal place—at the back of the bus.[2] Charles Taylor

1. In his masterful work, *A Secular Age*, Canadian philosopher Charles Taylor works through the impact of secularity comparing Western life in 1500 to 2000. Taylor explores secularity's impact in public spaces, decline in religious belief and practice, and the conditions of belief.

2. In his excellent work *Faith and the Public Square*, former Archbishop of Canterbury Rowan Williams makes the helpful distinction between procedural and programmatic secularism. Procedural secularism, the kind that I refer to above, is secularism that gives equal voices to all manner of religious and political thought. Programmatic secularism attempts to eliminate religious voices from the public realm and for that

notes that in the West, "the shift to secularity . . . consists . . . of a move from a society where belief in God is unchallenged and indeed, unproblematic, to one in which it is understood to be one option among others, and frequently not the easiest to embrace."[3] Some of us can still remember when secularism hit the school system. Growing up in western Canada, in the province of Manitoba, I recall my grade three teacher Ms. Duncan's final stand against secularism. Ms. Duncan (although she would have preferred to be called Mrs.) told stories of her days teaching in one-room prairie schoolhouses, still carried a ruler around the classroom for discipline, and was rumored to be 108 years old. Ms. Duncan was also a faithful member of her local Presbyterian church. When the government rules changed, no longer permitting religion in the classroom, Ms. Duncan just went on reading Scripture every morning as she had been taught eons ago in teacher's college (or "normal school" as they called it). She would also begin every day by having us stand beside our desks and recite the Lord's Prayer. When one young budding activist (perhaps his parents were lawyers!) challenged Ms. Duncan's insistence on saying the Lord's Prayer in a public school classroom, she responded to the student with grace and determination. "Well, class," she said in an even tone, "can anyone answer *why* we say the Lord's Prayer everyday?" Silence. Long pause. "Well, we say the Lord's Prayer day after day, until it lives inside us . . . until those words become a part of us. And one day, when you are older, and you are in trouble—you will *need* this prayer . . . you will need those words inside you. Your generation will need to work with God to make this world more like it is in heaven." I was too young at that time to know what the word "testimony" meant—but to this day I can still hear that saint testifying to her students about the power of public prayer.

Now, I am not going to debate the reality of secularism today. The "Ms. Duncans" of this world have long since passed or are no longer in public positions of influence in my post-Christendom Canadian context. Some might say that the battle for secularity was lost as early as the great "Lord's Day Alliance" movement of the early twentieth century when grim Protestants in dark suits protested street cars running on the Sabbath in Toronto. Denominations have floundered in their response to secularity as Walter Brueggemann so wisely noted nearly a quarter of a century ago:

Williams charges liberal modernity with being a fixed concept that approaches a new "pseudo-religion."

3. Taylor, *Secular Age*, 3.

On the surface, there is a drive for survival as mainline churches notice diminished membership, diminished dollars, and eroding influence and importance. Below that surface agenda, there is the growing awareness among us of the resistance of our culture to the primary culture of the gospel. That resistance takes the form of secularism, ofttimes expressed as indifference, and frequently evokes in response a kind of fearful legalism. It is clear, however, that the power of secularism is finally destructive, and that the re-action of legalism provides no adequate response or resolve on the part of the church. Beneath the growing awareness of that hostility to the gospel, moreover, there is the simple "news" of the gospel itself that provides a missionary impetus for sharing the news with our "news starved" society.[4]

There is growing acceptance, even amongst the formerly mainline denominations, that the Christendom privilege is over in North American society. Nevertheless, we must ask what we have exchanged a Christendom mind-set *for* instead. As Pope Francis suggested in the last chapter, our world is pervaded not only by secularism but consumerism.

Angus Reid, Vancouver resident and faithful supporter of Christ the Redeemer Catholic Church, is arguably Canada's best-known pollster. He said recently that, "Consumerism is the new religion." The number of Canadians who are "antireligious" has risen to 30 percent and another 40 percent are in the "muddled middle" in regards to spirituality. Young people are increasingly uninterested in prayer.[5] Now, let me be clear. I have no time for people who advance the mind-numbing argument that "things used to be better." Every generation thinks the next is going to "hell in a hand-basket." To believe that "things used to be better" is to long for a past century that included world wars, racism, colonialism, sexism, and any other number of grievous sins. The reality of sin is constant, just as God's victory over sin on the cross is assured. The question that begs asking is, "What does God demand from *this* generation of believers?"

If secularity + individualism + consumerism is the new contextual normal for Christ followers in North America, what then is our next most faithful step? It seems delicious to me when so many people quote the mantra of "secularity" as being the division or separation of church and state. We even have a delightful vineyard close to home called Church and State—it's

---

4. Brueggemann, *Biblical Perspectives on Evangelism*, 7.
5. Douglas Todd, "Angus Reid, Unchained," *Vancouver Sun Blog*, June, 19, 2015.

just down the road from Blasted Church Vineyards, a whole other story.[6] To take even a cursory glance at the history of New England Puritanism with its larger-than-life characters like John Cotton or Increase Mathers or Jonathan Edwards is to understand that the language of "separation of church and state" was for a totally different reason. Fleeing persecution in Europe for their Reformed Christian views, the Puritans established their "city on a hill" in order to protect the church *from* the state—not, as it is commonly assumed today, out of a need to protect the state from the church.

With a gentle nod to our Puritan ancestors, it would serve us well to acknowledge the challenge of secularity and consumerism in the dominant culture of affluence and ask what the gospel calls us, as a minority, to do in response. Richard Bauckham cautions, "Christians should not be seduced by the enticing notion that economic growth as such is self-evidently a prime good for humanity. We must probe the facts behind this glib assumption and ask questions about who and what is benefited or damaged by the actual economic growth that we are considering."[7] For decades now Christian missiologists have been sounding alarm bells regarding the disease of the adoption of Western culture into the church. Stanley Hauerwas and Will Willimon in their classic 1989 work *Resident Aliens: Life in the Christian Colony,* picked up on Lesslie Newbigin's early missional work that served as a "canary in the coal mine" for the so-called mainline church. Reflecting on the impact of *Resident Aliens,* Willimon said,

> The book announced, although we didn't put it this way at the time, that sentimental, subjective, squeamish Docetism is a greater peril for North American Christians than arrogant ecclesiastical triumphalism. Our line was not drawn between righteousness and sin, or belief and atheism, or liberalism and conservatism but between the church and the world.[8]

More recently, Ross Hastings has cautioned against the church's missiological turn in North America that may have started with inculturation but has ended with enculturation. Inculturation is a missiological term "which refers to ways to adapt the communication of the gospel for a specific culture being evangelized."[9] Enculturation, on the other hand, is a process of influence by the dominant culture upon "an individual or community

6. www.churchandstatewines.com and www.blastedchurch.com
7. Bauckham, *Bible and Mission,* 94.
8. Hauerwas and Willimon, *Resident Aliens,* 5.
9. Hastings, *Missional God, Missional Church,* 38.

(e.g., the church) to imbibe its accepted norms and values so the individual or community is pressured to find acceptance within the society of that culture."[10] Hastings balances the positive aspects of culture (creation of humankind in the image of God) with the demonic corruption of culture (the fall of humankind) on the other. He names the tension by stating, "the challenge the Western church faces is that it is often encultured in ways that it ought not to be, and that it is not inculturating the gospel in ways it ought to be."[11] When we speak of "domesticating the gospel" we are referring to this "indiscriminate enculturation" that Hastings names in the Western church, whereby, "instead of speaking and acting prophetically against such elements of culture, the church can easily become inappropriately enculturated and swamped with the waters of insidious influences incompatible with the gospel."[12]

When I was a graduate student in Toronto, I had a beloved classmate from Newfoundland who, when she was "losing" a theological argument in seminary, would invoke the phrase meant to end debate, "Don't make baby Jesus cry." There was something so precious about that. Of course, she used that phrase "tongue in cheek" with a twinkle in her eye but there is more truth in that phrase than first meets the eye. It would be years later when Will Ferrell starred in his epic NASCAR movie, *Talladega Nights: The Ballad of Ricky Bobby*. In one priceless scene Will Ferrell's character is sitting down to dinner with his family and offers a revealing grace. Ricky Bobby prays to baby Jesus for the bountiful harvest of Domino's, Kentucky Fried Chicken, and Taco Bell. He thanks baby Jesus for his handsome sons Walker and Texas Ranger and then asks for healing for his father-in-law's smelly and infected leg. Ricky Bobby's "smoking hot" wife Carly interrupts the grace to inform Ricky Bobby that, in fact, Jesus did grow up and that there is no need to keep calling him a baby. And then, in the line that summarizes all that is wrong with a gospel domesticated by a culture of secularity, individualism, and consumerism Ricky Bobby replies that he likes the Christmas Jesus best, so that's who he is going to pray to. If the other people around the dining room table have a Jesus they prefer like grown-up Jesus or bearded Jesus then they should feel free to pray to him instead. Classic.

I remember showing that clip to a congregation I served in Ontario on Christmas Eve. It was an invitation to reflect on that warm feeling that

10. Ibid. 38.
11. Ibid.
12. Ibid. 39.

comes so naturally at Christmastime (often aided by a spiked eggnog before church!). Of course, we celebrate the incarnation of Christ—but as part of God's sovereign plan of salvation for the whole world. The reason the Puritans in New England cancelled Christmas was not because of a weak incarnational theology, but rather because they were convinced that Christmas would be commercialized. Oh those silly Puritans. Consumerism, individualism, and secularity all work in our day to domesticate the gospel. These less than subtle forces at work in our lives are trying to convert us from the robust, life-changing gospel of the risen Christ to a toothless, cultural Christianity. Domesticating the gospel in the mainline church in North America has been easy. After all, we have served as coconspirators. Over the last twenty-five years, many churches have paid more attention to their declining numbers playing the "nickels and noses" game rather than shaping "missional disciples" to evangelize the world. "Don't rock the boat" has become "Don't rock the cradle" in a time and place where we cloak failure in the language of faithfulness and try our best to not make "baby Jesus cry."

What does this actually look like theologically in our churches when we succumb to the pressures of the consumerist, individualist, and secularize culture around us? Moralistic. Therapeutic. Deism. Princeton scholar Kenda Dean introduced many of us through her writing to sociologist Christian Smith, who coined the phrase "Moralistic Therapeutic Deism" to describe the default religion taught to teenagers in American churches.[13] When I had dinner recently at Kenda's house at Princeton Theological Seminary she said that she did not think that the language of "Moralistic Therapeutic Deism" would be accessible enough for most people. She learned early on, however, that "MTD" spoke so honestly of the theological malaise in mainline Protestantism that people in pulpit and pew were soon using the language themselves to describe what had gone wrong in practical theology. After all, this kind of milquetoast theology produces malnourished disciples who flounder in such a strong consumerist culture where one is easily swayed to pay attention to profits rather than pray attention to prophets.

13. From the National Study of Youth and Religion, Moralistic Therapeutic Deism can be summarized by the following statements: 1. A god exists who created and ordered the world and watches over human life on earth. 2. God wants people to be good, nice, and fair to each other, as taught in the Bible and by most world religions. 3. The central goal of life is to be happy and to feel good about oneself. 4. God does not need to be particularly involved in one's life except when God is needed to resolve a problem. 5. Good people go to heaven when they die.

A decade before Ricky Bobby roared onto the scene in *Talladega Nights*, a wonderful Christian scholar was already attending to the domestication of the gospel in Western culture from his modest office at Wabash College. William Placher published his profound work *The Domestication of Transcendence*. In it, Placher explores the classic teaching of Aquinas, Luther, and Calvin, affirming that, despite their differences, they shared a belief in a transcendent yet immanent God who could not be understood in human categories. The shift to modernity brought with it the unfortunate attempts to categorize and comprehend the Divine under the microscope of human reason. God has been "reduced" and the result of the shift is the domestication of transcendence. The living God revealed in Jesus Christ cannot be studied like a cadaver in a morgue. As Placher argues:

> Human reason cannot figure its way to such a God, since a God we could figure out, a God fitted to the categories of our understanding, would therefore not be transcendent in an appropriately radical sense. We can know the transcendent God not as an object within our intellectual grasp but only as a self-revealing subject, and even our knowledge of divine self-revelation must itself be God's doing. Christian faith finds here confirmation of God's Triune character: We come to know this gracious God not merely in revelation but in self-revelation in Jesus Christ, and we come to trust that we do know God in Christ through the work of the Holy Spirit.[14]

The domestication of the gospel is so strong in our North American culture that it is not even difficult to spot within Christian community. Those who seek to respond to God in Christ find themselves translating the gospel into a culture that is crafty and cunning. As Darrell Guder warns, "Cultures try to bring the gospel under their control, attempting to fit the person and work of Jesus Christ into their patterns of accepted religious practice. Translation is a risk, and thus the process must be of continuing conversion."[15] Our ongoing conversion is absolutely critical if we are to receive the grace-filled gift to see the culture around us for what it really is, rather than what it seeks to sell us on. As Guder contends, "The witnesses are always very ambiguous saints. They (we) never divorce themselves from the desire to bring this powerful and radical gospel under control."[16]

14. Placher, *Domestication of Transcendence*, 182.
15. Guder, *Continuing Conversion*, 85.
16. Ibid., 97.

What might (re)conversion look like for us as missionary disciples as we seek to respond faithfully to the pervasive and corrupting power of the consumerist, individualistic and secularized culture in North America today? Having acknowledged our sin of pride in the previous chapter, it now falls to us to confess that our sin of envy helps us domesticate the claims of the gospel, in order to live as we might choose rather than how God would have us be in community.

I remember reading years ago one of those great cartoons that appear in each issue of *The New Yorker* magazine. The scene was of two women sitting having a cup of tea when one says to the other, "I envy you—I wish I was close enough to my family to be estranged." Envy is part of the human experience. It drives us to say and do terrible things that bring harm to others as well as ourselves. A quick glance at the book of Genesis alone reveals countless stories where envy leads to disaster. Adam and Eve are envious that God has access to the knowledge of good and evil. That ends in disaster. Cain is envious of Abel's flocks. That ends in death. People build the tower of Babel envious of God's reputation and fame. That ends in debacle. Sarah is envious of how Abraham looks at Hagar's son Ishmael over Isaac. That ends in departing. Jacob is envious of Esau's birthright. That leads to division. Joseph's brothers are envious of his special attention and snappy coat. That leads to dispatching. And so it goes. But going into a little more detail is helpful if we are to repent of our own envy and be converted again and again to the power of the gospel.

Let's go back to Abraham and Sarah. They long for a child but once they start collecting their old age security it doesn't look like children are in the cards. And then three angels visit them and by "entertaining angels unaware," as the book of Hebrews puts it, they are blessed with the good news of a child. Indeed, in her old age Sarah gives birth to Isaac, reminding the reader of the biblical claim that with God all things are possible. Isaac ends up with Rebekah after Abraham's servant presents her in Genesis 24 not with the traditional engagement ring from the local shopping mall diamond store but with a nose ring—a great youth group Bible study! Isaac and Rebekah have two sons—Jacob and Esau, the twins that were wrestling even in the womb. Not a good sign. Well, they fight just as much as they grow up and the brothers are estranged over a birthright and a cup of soup from the ancient world's equivalent of Whole Foods. Jacob takes off to his house of his Uncle Laban (who was there the night the engagement . . . I mean nose . . . ring was presented to Rebekah). Jacob finds not only one nice girl in town, but after a little wedding night trick, two—Leah *and* Rachel. Can anyone say dysfunctional family? Well, it gets worse. Leah has no trouble having children and lords it over Rachel. Rachel is—wait for it—*envious* and retaliates by offering Jacob her female servant and they have a child. Servants are traded back and forth, Jacob fathers children with a number of women—it's like something from a soap opera. In the end, Rachel finally conceives and has a son—Joseph. Ah, now you see where we are going here.

Jacob wrestles an angel, makes peace with his brother Esau, and settles down back home for a quiet domestic life. Sort of. The trouble is the dysfunctional family moves down a generation. No longer is it Jacob and Esau fighting—they've made their peace. Now it is Jacob's own children—his twelve boys—that have a conflict.

Jacob favors Joseph and gives him a famous coat of many colors. That makes Joseph's brothers *envious*. That, and Joseph's dream interpretation that has his family bowing down before him doesn't help things much either. One day when Joseph went out into the fields wearing his flashy new coat, his brothers decided to kill him. Indeed, it appears that the sin of envy is deadly. But his one brother, the first-born Reuben, has a guilty conscience. Who would have thought that the guy named after a sandwich would be the hero? Better than mock chicken or bologna, I guess. He says, "Hey guys, why kill our brother Joseph when we could sell him and make some money?" Nice touch.

They throw Joseph down a cistern and wait for the first caravan passing by to make a deal. I've stood in one of those traditional cisterns in Israel. The one I was in dated from the time of King Solomon, although the way cisterns were built did not change a great deal over time. Carved from rock in a cross formation to keep them from caving in, they were designed to collect rainwater for the use of humans and animals. Thankfully, the Bible says the cistern that Joseph was thrown into was empty.

What do we make of this curious story? Is envy really that deadly? While we may want to downplay envy, philosophers and other thinkers have long warned of the power of envy. Immanuel Kant called envy a natural impulse intent on the destruction of others. Lord Chesterfield explained envy by saying that people hate those who make them feel their own inferiority. Perhaps the most helpful comment for me is from the Christian philosopher Soren Kierkegaard, who argued that envy takes the form of leveling. In other words, envy drives people to pull others down. It's like those games at the local fairgrounds called Whac-A-Mole," where the mole pops up and you have to smack it down. Instead of celebrating a colleague's success there is often a knee-jerk reaction to cut the person down—envy appears to have an odd praise for mediocrity. But why?

It seems like self-pity asks the question, "Why me?" while envy begs the question, "Why *not* me?" Envy invites us to look at our neighbor with scorn and ask, "Why do I *not* have as nice a job, home, spouse, children?" on and on. Envy leads us to ask, "Why did I *not* get that attention, vacation, bonus, promotion, or honor?" Envy drives us to look with resentment upon others around us and to take joy only in their humbling. As Joseph Epstein writes,

> Of the seven deadly sins, only envy is no fun at all. Sloth may not seem much fun, nor anger either, but giving way to deep laziness has its pleasures and the expression of anger entails a release that is not without its small delights. In recompense, envy may be the subtlest—perhaps I should say the most insidious—of the seven deadly sins. Surely it is the one that people are least likely to want to own up to, for to do so is to admit that one is probably ungenerous, mean, small-hearted. It may also be the most endemic.[17]

As disciples of Christ envy has no place in our daily lives and practice of the gospel. Jesus says, "Anyone who wants to be first must be the very last, and the servant of all."[18] In Matthew 20 Jesus tells the parable of the workers in the vineyard and reveals how humankind is envious even of God's generosity. Our envious nature is revealed as in the famous line from Gore Vidal, "Every time a friend succeeds, I die a little." Sadly, it is clear how domesticating the gospel is required in order for us to wiggle free from the demands of loving our neighbor and praying for our enemies.

Thank God, literally, that as we read through this story of envy in the book of Genesis we discover that despite the power of sin, the Lord has the ability to transform even the deepest held jealousy and scorn. By Genesis 42, when there is a famine in the land, Joseph's brothers are sent to Egypt to buy food for their hungry family. They come into Joseph's presence, but do not recognize their brother in all his finery and authority (Joseph even uses an interpreter but knows what they are saying). Here it is—envy's revenge. Joseph has the power to crush his enemies to gain revenge over those who did him harm. And yet, God melts his heart and moves him

17. Epstein, *Envy*, 1.
18. Mark 9:35, *NIV.*

with compassion. He calls for the one brother left behind—Benjamin—his only full brother (son of Rachel) and the family is reunited, forgiven, blessed. Even ambiguous saints can be (re)converted. The sovereignty of God can, and will, overcome our envious and selfish desires to domesticate the gospel and lacquer a thin veneer of religiosity over our attempts to keep baby Jesus from crying out for justice and righteousness. The gospel has the power, when it is proclaimed in freedom and truth, to be the Holy Spirit's reconciling agent in the world. What would our worshipping communities look like set free to share the love of the God of Israel we know through the life, death, and resurrection of Jesus still at work in this world, in our lives?

Turning envy into an embrace
Jealousy into justice
Covetousness into charity.

Chapter Four

Here I Am to Worship
(the Unholy Trinity of Me, Myself, and I)

Many churches of all persuasions are hiring research agencies to poll neighborhoods, asking what kind of church they prefer. Then the local churches design themselves to fit the desires of the people. True faith in God that demands selflessness is being replaced by trendy religion that serves the selfish.

—Billy Graham

"I need to speak to you this week," the church member said, a certain urgency in his voice. "Sure," I replied in the midst of shaking hands after Sunday worship, "How about Tuesday at 10 AM?" Two days later, I was busily working away at some correspondence when my secretary knocked and said that my 10 AM appointment had arrived. I welcomed the gentleman into my office and sat down across from him, eager to hear what he had to say. "How can I help you today?" I asked the man as he shifted his weight uneasily in the chair. "Well, I've got a problem," the man said flatly, "and it's not just me." "All right," I replied, "what seems to be your problem?" "Well, it's your preaching around here—these past few years." "Oh," I said, my eyebrows rising. "Your preaching is making a lot of us uncomfortable." Silence. "You mention sin a lot more than previous preachers and you talk about Jesus like you really *believe* in him." "Yeah," I nodded, slightly confused where this conversation was going. "Well," the man paused, flushing red with anger, "you need to know that I've done a lot around this church (insert a long list of leadership roles and responsibilities the man held in the congregation) and worship around here makes me uncomfortable these days." "How so?" I replied. "Well, worship and your preaching makes it sound like we need to believe in Jesus or something. I didn't sign on for that." Awkward silence. In a more belligerent tone he continued, "You need to know that many of us don't believe any of this faith sh*t. We just come here because we like singing in the choir and listening to the classical music on the organ." "Well," I replied more calmly than I should have, "it sounds like you need to go home and pray about this." And with that, the man stood up and stormed out of the office. Lord, have mercy.

In a post-Christendom North America, Christ followers encounter people of no expressed belief and all kinds of different beliefs everyday. The interactions we have with others as apologists can range from angry atheists to affable agnostics to the amiable apathetic folks whose Sunday ritual includes visiting Starbucks and reading *The New York Times* religiously. Today, however, we also deal with a number of "cultural Christians" many of whom were raised in an era when to be a good citizen and to be a good Christian went hand in hand. These are the kind of folks who introduce you to their "witty, secular" friends and then say in a hushed tone, "they would be a good and generous church member, you should tell them about what the church can do to meet their needs." These are the folks who arm twist their clergy and churches into accepting a domestication of transcendence and feel free to be Marcion-like, playing "cut and paste" with the Scriptures, until they have a gospel gutted of obedience to Christ and missing God's call to transform the world—beginning with us.[1] It does not take long to link this unholy Trinity of "me, myself, and I" in the church to the dominant culture of affluence and consumerism all around our places of worship. As Soong-Chan Rah describes,

1. Marcion, a preacher's kid and wealthy businessperson, is one of my favorite early church heretics who in the second century felt totally at liberty to cut out the Old/First Testament from the canon as well as a good portion of the New Testament, sticking with the Gospel of Luke and some of Paul's letters. His movement continued for several centuries as a rival to the orthodox teaching of the mainstream church. He was perhaps the best early church example of the unholy Trinity of "me, myself, and I."

Materialism, however, is not limited to what we physically own as churches (such as our buildings) but also extends to our mindset and approach to church life. Because of our materialistic bent and our consumer mentality, our spirituality can become shallow. When life is reduced to a materialistic exchange of goods, our spiritual life can also be reduced to an exchange of goods. Spiritual life becomes a consumable product that is exchanged only if it benefits the material and corporal well-being of the individual consumer. We begin to think of ourselves as consumer when we relate to our local church.[2]

Rather than understanding the church as the sent people of God, as missionary disciples who are deployed to bless and mend God's broken world as witnesses to resurrection power, too often we have encouraged and enabled an entitlement mentality regarding membership in the church. This lingering postwar 1950s model of membership church, that existed primarily to meet the needs of those consumers in the pews rather than those outside the walls of the church, is an ongoing obstacle to missional practice in the mainline church. This membership model all too often "outsources its baptismal vows" to paid clergy and feels that showing up through "noses and nickels" is all that is required. As Michael Foss argued in *Power Surge,* too many mainline Protestant churches approach their ministry like belonging to a health club. Foss illustrates his thesis like this:

> One becomes a member of a health club by paying dues (in a church, the monthly or weekly offering). Having paid their dues, the members expect the services of the club to be at their disposal. Exercise equipment, weight room, aerobics classes, an indoor track, swimming pool—all there for them, with a trained staff to see that they benefit by them. Members may bring a guest on occasion, but only those who pay their dues have a right to the use of the facilities and the attention of the staff. There is no need to belabor the point. Many of the people who sit in the pews on Sunday have come to think of church membership in ways analogous to how the fitness crowd views membership in a health club.[3]

What's surprising, however, is that most of us would feel cheated if we paid for a gym membership and showed up once a week to watch other people use the equipment while we sat there and stared. How strange! Surely, the purpose of the gymnasium is for us to exercise and, if the church is like a

2. Rah, *Next Evangelicalism,* 54.

3. Foss, *Power Surge,* 15.

gymnasium, for us to stretch our sanctified lives further for the sake of the kingdom. That's why I'm not entirely sure the gymnasium is the best analogy. I wonder if a movie theatre or even a street performer might be a more suitable fit. For some, church simply becomes a performance they attend. If it no longer suits their personal desires, then they move on to another performance. In the movement from a parish-based approach to church to the commuter model or "voluntary society," people pass many mission communities on their way to a "church of their choice" each week.[4] This "consumerist" model of Christianity certainly mirrors the consumerist culture of North America where people use their freedom to flow easily from one service provider or product to another based on their personal preference or the most desirable price. What could be better than a "low-cost" (to you), high-attraction church for many people? The freedom to move between churches based on personal preference has become an assumed fact of Christian lifestyle in North America today. We even tell jokes like the shipwrecked man rescued on a deserted island. The rescuers compliment the man on the three huts that he built over his years on the island. "Yes," the man replies, "that hut on the left is my home and that hut on the right is my church." Confused, the rescuers ask, "And what is that hut in the middle?" "Oh," the man replies, "that's the church *that I used to go to.*"

Missional leadership today has to discern how much of the "Christendom mind-set" to engage and how much energy to invest in those who "think they are Christian" but who bought into the cheap grace that was on offer in previous years. It's a little bit like the older woman who lingered after shaking hands one Sunday at church. "Hi there, thanks for worshipping today. I'm not sure I've had the pleasure of meeting you before," I said. "Oh, I'm just visiting. I used to be a member here years ago but I moved to a different city." "Welcome back," I said cheerfully, "what was it like worshipping again in this place?" "Oh, just fine, thank you," she said casually. "I do miss the days of Rev. (insert Christendom-loving minister with an "old country" accent here) when the church was full." I nodded and she continued, "Oh, how I loved his preaching. He used to tell the best fireside stories each Sunday without mentioning the Bible—and he got away with it! Isn't that wonderful?" she said with a cackle. I was momentarily speechless. I doubted that was entirely true of the beloved "Christendom minister" but was shocked nonetheless that a parishioner would remember weekly proclamation in such a way. Finally I recovered and said in an even tone,

4. Guder, *Continuing Conversion,* 146–47.

"No, I don't think that's wonderful. In fact, I feel sorry for you. You were cheated out of an experience of the life-changing gospel." She frowned and walked away.

Rather than driving all over town in search of a performance, missional leadership is encouraging Christians to attend more closely to their neighborhood as a place where God sends us to engage in witness and action for the sake of the gospel. Colleagues at the nearby Seattle School of Theology and Psychology, for example, have teamed up with the Parish Collective to offer instruction on how to counter this decades-long slide of "commuter church."[5] Quoting psychologist Christina Cleveland, the Parish Collective notes that when church left its historical focus within the neighborhood it ended up becoming homogeneous and consumer-orientated so that "today's churchgoers . . . tend to shop for churches that express their individual values and are culturally similar. We often drive by dozens of churches, the one that meets our cultural expectations . . . that some scholars pejoratively call 'Burger King Christianity.'"[6] *The New Parish* pushes back against the assumption that church means "showing up to a weekly performance" while "composing and maintaining a shiny, happy disposition" and "consuming the services of a professionalized ministry."[7]

The classic "pushback" against this reduction of church to "consuming religion" in mainline Protestantism is to season our "churchy vocabulary" with social justice terms. Missional theology is careful, however, to distinguish between acts of charity or the pronouncement of the "right" viewpoint on any given topic, compared to the messiness of entering into *relationship* with our neighbors all around whether they are engaged in our local church or not. *The Art of Neighboring* is a helpful addition to the missional literature in this regard, since it is trying to redefine what mission and ministry look like in a post-Christendom context.[8] Jay Pathak and Dave Runyon have mapped out a practical, hands-on approach for living out the Great Commandment by loving God and neighbor that begins with an acknowledgement that isolation, fear, and misunderstanding keep many

---

5. *The New Parish* is a theologically rich and missionally focused work by Paul Sparks, Tim Soerens, and Dwight J. Friesen describing their work on being a mission community in Seattle.

6. Sparks, Soerens, and Friesen, eds., *New Parish*, 25.

7. Ibid., 76.

8. *The Art of Neighboring* is another work that is reshaping our sense of local mission and challenging Christians to build relationships with those who live around them and not just those who share the same worship space.

neighbors as strangers in North America today. Pathak and Runyon warn that like the lawyer who sparks the parable of the Good Samaritan we are often looking for a loophole in North America today to take Jesus' teaching seriously. They caution:

> If we say, "Everyone is my neighbor," it can become an excuse for avoiding the implications of following the Great Commandment. Our "neighbors" become defined in the broadest of terms. They're the people across town, the people who are helped by the organizations that receive our donations, the people whom the government helps. We don't have to feel guilty, we tell ourselves. After all, we can't be expected to really love everybody, can we? The problem is, however, that when we aim for everything, we hit nothing. So when we insist we're neighbors with everybody, often we end up being neighbors with nobody. That's our human nature. We become like the lawyer looking for a loophole. We tell ourselves that we've got a lot going on in our lives, so surely the Great Commandment applies only to the wounded enemy across many of those lately, surely we're doing just fine when it comes to loving our neighbors. Maybe not.[9]

To test one's engagement with his or her neighbors, Pathak and Runyon developed a chart to help move the Great Commandment from a theory into a real-world context by having people identify the eight "neighbors" around their home or apartment. The first step is simple. Can you write the names of the people who live in the houses around you? Even writing first names only is acceptable. The second step is to write down relevant information about the people who live in the eight homes around that you could not tell by simply seeing them in the driveway or apartment hallway. For example, write down where they are from and what kind of work they do. Third, write down in-depth information that might include a sense of their dreams and goals and purpose for life. Based on your conversations with them what do they believe and according to what values do they live their lives? In sharing this exercise with church people Pathak and Runyon have discovered that about 10 percent of people can fill out the names of all eight neighbors, 3 percent can fill out the second question for everyone and only 1 percent can fill out the deeper third question for each home.[10] *The Art of Neighboring* pushes us beyond our comfortable default position

9. Pathak and Runyon, *Art of Neighboring*, 35.

10. Ibid., 39.

best captured in the line from Charlie Brown, "I love humanity, it's people I can't stand."

Missional leadership rejects the fraud of "cultural Christianity" that defines church by consuming a religious event once a week and sets the bar much higher when it comes to our love of God and neighbor. Commitment to Christ and neighbor are expected and such relationships require "frequency of contact and communication, common worship and Christian activity, and mutual responsibility and support. Incarnational witness happens in the specific and concrete actions and relationships of intentional communities."[11] Missional leadership brokers no deal with "cultural Christianity" that demands little and enables "members" to ask much of "professional clergy." No, Missional leadership in a culture of affluence expects that "followers of Jesus want to be the church together in deeper ways than simply attending professionalized church programs" and seeks to integrate mission, community, and discipleship into a life that holistically worships the Triune God following Jesus in the neighborhood.[12] In fact, as Michael Frost states, "Missional Leaders don't see changing the church as central to their cause; they want to change the whole world."[13] Participating in the Missio Dei that Frost calls "the unstoppable program of God's unfurling kingdom on earth," missional leaders cannot "even conceive of how to control it, package it, or franchise it."[14]

We spoke in an earlier chapter about the ever-present danger of idolatry. The old lie from the garden that if we can only "hip check" God out of here, we will be godlike ourselves. Missional leadership needs to address the pervasive worship of the unholy Trinity of "me, myself, and I" running rampant in North American "selfie" culture by establishing new or renewing missional communities that focus on worship, witness and work.

Two local mission communities recently helped me understand what it looks like to be a people gathered around worship, witness, and work. University Presbyterian Church in Seattle is known for its effective and faithful ministry in the Pacific Northwest. Several years ago, the elders of the congregation felt God calling them to plant a new mission community. They were called to purchase a warehouse in the South Lake Union neighborhood of Seattle. Urban planners in the congregation told the session

---

11. Guder, *Continuing Conversion*, 148–49.

12. Sparks, Soerens, and Friesen, eds., *New Parish*, 139 and 190.

13. Frost, *Road to Missional*, 21.

14. Ibid.

that this was the next up-and-coming neighborhood in the city. The church commissioned its well-loved youth and young adult ministers, James B. and Renee Notkin, to minister in that community.[15] James B. and Renee established a coffee shop and set to work on building relationships in the community. Like the Apostle Paul, James B. had a varied skill set that included business and theology. His "tentmaking" skills helped establish a thriving coffee shop in one-third of the building and a gathering space for worship, witness, and work in the remaining two-thirds of the space. In time, the urban planners were proved right as Amazon established its world headquarters in South Lake Union—and the place came alive. Soon "Union Church" as it was called became the hottest nonprofit space in a growing neighborhood of young executives living in loft apartments or shiny new condo towers. James B. varies the Sunday gathering with a mix of worship, witness, and work. Some Sundays, people gather for an uplifting worship service of praise. Other Sundays, a brief worship turns into a Bible study with small groups where people do the heavy lifting of Scripture together. Still other Sundays, a brief worship is followed by an invitation for disciples to sign up for one of several activities of service in the community that morning—everything from cleaning up trash to making sandwiches at the local homeless shelter to visiting in a nearby nursing home. James B. has told me that several people have come into a relationship with Christ who were suspicious of Christians but came at first on the Sundays where they could serve in the community. We've adopted this format for our own chapel services where I teach at the University of British Columbia. Missional worship terrifies and electrifies students and faculty alike as we go forth from St. Andrew's Hall to serve and witness to God's glory on campus.

Another mission community that has encouraged me lately is St. Peter's Fireside in downtown Vancouver. A new mission community, it is an outreach in the downtown to so many who live in the skyscraper condos yet who describe isolation from neighbors as one of the biggest obstacles to urban living.[16] In fact, Vancouver is home to an incredible number of church plants—missional leaders who are trying to figure out what God is up to in a community with so many pre-Christians that presenting the

15. Union Church serves as an encouraging example of a mission community with a focus on worship, witness, and work: www.unionchurchseattle.org.

16. This isolation for young urbanites was the focus of a major report funded by the Vancouver Foundation entitled *Connected and Engaged*. It is especially good reading for those trying to practice Missional Leadership in an urban context: https://www.vancouverfoundation.ca/initiatives/connections-and-engagement.

gospel here feels a lot like standing on Mars Hill with Paul in Acts 17. The mission community uses excellent online tools to engage with their young, wired congregation. Participation in a mission community like this leaves no room for spectators or those who have settled for consumerist religion with its "outsourcing of baptismal vows" to paid clergy. Spending time in mission communities like Union Church or St. Peter's Fireside makes me hopeful and exciting for what the Holy Spirit is doing in our midst.

Perhaps the most exciting part of these new and (re)newed mission communities emerging in our post-Christendom context is that there is less and less room for folks who want to observe the "Sunday show" or take out the membership but never exercise on the ecclesiastical elliptical machine or the sanctified spin bike. Years ago I met one of our "Alumni Association" members of the church at a funeral reception. You know, those social settings where weak coffee and sandwiches with the crusts cut off are served. Where do those crusts go anyways? I introduced myself to a person standing by herself and she told me, "I used to go to your church." "Is that right?" I said with mild interest. "Yeah, we once belonged here but my husband was transferred to another city and we moved our membership." "But you are back now in the neighborhood?" I inquired. "Oh yes," she replied in a clipped tone, "we moved back a couple of years ago." Sensing she was on a roll, she said, "We called to transfer our membership back here but I was told by your secretary that we'd have to stand up at the front on a membership Sunday and confess our faith in Jesus." "Yes . . . ," I said cautiously, sensing this story had layers to it, "that's right, we like to celebrate new and returning members with the congregation and together rededicate our lives to the Lord." "Well, I just told your secretary I wasn't going to do that." Pastorally, I said, "Oh, are you uncomfortable standing up in front of large numbers of people?" "No, don't be silly," she said, "I speak in front of crowds all the time." Really confused now, I said, "Well, what was the problem?" She replied sardonically, "Well I made a confession of faith a long time ago when I was a teenager during confirmation at the cathedral. How ridiculous! How many times do you have to confess your faith in Jesus, really?" I blinked and took a breath. "Well, we are recovering sinners, so I suppose we need to confess the Lordship of Christ everyday—sometimes multiple times in the day. It would be like a husband saying to his wife, 'I told you I loved you once on our wedding day and I don't need to ever say it again.'" She snorted. "Well, I don't know about that. Besides, we called another church in the neighborhood and they were more than happy to take our membership—and pledge—without asking us to do a thing." She turned on her heels, teacup and crustless sandwich in hand, and walked away.

Today, the Holy Spirit is shaping and equipping mission communities to be places so different than Christendom's "country clubs of religion." Cultural Christianity, of the Laodicean kind, cannot die fast enough and churches that ask nothing of their disciples but promise to serve their member's every needs will one day face an accounting of that heretical practice. In a culture of affluence there will always be a seductive pull towards the unholy worship of me, myself, and I. For those daring enough to respond to God's call and serve as missional leaders, advice from the Old Testament like "gird your loins" comes to mind. As Lesslie Newbigin cautions,

> Ministerial leadership for a missionary congregation will require that the minister is directly engaged in the warfare of the kingdom against the powers which usurp the kingship. . . . There will be situations where the minister must represent the whole Church in challenging abuse of power, corruption, and selfishness in public life and take the blows that follow. As he or she does this, the way will be open for standing in solidarity with members of the congregation who have to face similar conflict. There is a sense in which the Christian warfare against the world, the flesh, and the devil is all one warfare. Those who display courage in one sector of the line encourage everyone. The minister will encourage the whole company by the courage with which he or she engages the enemy. And, of course, as Paul reminds us, "the weapons of our warfare are not worldly but have divine power to destroy strongholds" (2 Cor. 10: 4). The minister's leadership of the congregation in its mission to the world will be first and foremost in the area of his or her own discipleship, in that life of prayer and daily consecration which remains hidden from the world but which is the place where the essential battles are either won or lost. . . . Ministerial leadership is, first and finally, discipleship.[17]

Missional leaders are sent into a culture of affluence to speak up and speak out against the demonizing lure of self-worship with joyful praise of the Triune God. Missional leadership confesses, "I'm (not) sorry" as it stirs up Christian apologetics (defense of the faith) for apologetic Christians, who are sent forth to counter the consumerist mind-set with a confession of faith in the living God. This proclamation, however, is not of the doom

17. Newbigin, *The Gospel in a Pluralist Society*, 240–41.

and gloom variety. No, we proclaim God's grace and goodness against the powers and principalities of this world knowing that in the cross of Christ, God's victory has already been achieved over sin and death. Our turn from self-worship (which ultimately ends in self-loathing) to the genuine praise of the Triune God is a movement full of joy and thanksgiving. As I heard Willie Jennings from Duke Divinity School once warn, "To say you must first love yourself before you can love your neighbor is to commit yourself to solitary confinement." There is nothing more freeing than knowing that God is God and we are not. Commenting on Karl Barth's theology, Christopher Green says

> On the side of the creature, doxology is a final victory over evil because it is a turning against the last temptation that she will face: the enticement to think that she can, in any way, contribute to the glory of God with her own praise. Barth avoids this temptation by simply extolling God; this means that he does not attempt to explain too much. To ascribe, "Kingdom, power and glory" to God in doxology is to overcome any confusion about the importance of one's own praise.[18]

Missional leadership reminds us, by grace, both who and whose we are. As the old revivalist preacher Charles Spurgeon once said in his sermon "All of Grace," "A child of God should be a visible Beatitude, for joy and happiness, and a living Doxology, for gratitude and adoration." Therefore, missional leadership is by its very nature doxological inviting us with joyful hearts to proclaim:

> Praise God from whom all blessings flow;
> Praise him, all creatures here below;
> Praise him above, ye heavenly host:
> Praise Father, Son, and Holy Ghost.

---

18. Green, *Doxological Theology*, 188–89.

Chapter Five

Full of It?
Beyond Bankrupting Functional Atheism

You cannot serve two masters.
Either you will hate the one and love the other or you will be devoted to the one
and despise the other. You cannot serve both God and money.

—Matthew 6:24

Thus far, we've explored the particular and peculiar challenge of missional leadership in a North American culture of affluence. Like the Laodiceans in the book of Revelation, many in North America live in great luxury compared to the rest of the world, yet the sin of envy, combined with pride, holds us back from naming our own despair and denial as Laodicean captive Christians. To borrow Darrell Guder's language, every culture must engage in reduction of the gospel in order to translate it from one context to another (Israel to Hellenistic, Hellenistic to Roman, etc.). The problem comes when reduction includes our sinful desire to control and domesticate the gospel. Reduction + control, according to Guder, equals *reductionism*, whereby the changes we make to the gospel, in order to communicate evangelistically, are tainted by human sin and take on an alien, authoritative, and absolutist form. The earlier example of the man who felt that attending church solely involved a love of classical music, without a daily acknowledgment of living under the Lordship of Jesus Christ, would serve as an example.

Before we turn to the second half of this work and joyfully lean into the prompting of the Holy Spirit to leave Laodicea behind, we first must go even deeper into naming the impact that affluence has had on the reductionism of the gospel in North American Christianity. We have already illustrated the danger that the sins of idolatry, pride, and envy play in maintaining the Laodicean captivity of the church today. There are more sins just beneath the surface, however, which this affluent reductionism of the gospel feeds in North America today—and we're full of them.

A few years ago I was captivated by a show produced by a bunch of guys in Montreal called Epic Meal Time. Essentially, the whole idea of the show revolves around men making the most gluttonous meals you can imagine. For example, one Super Bowl weekend they made a 100,000-calorie cheeseburger and then ate it. For a "healthy" change, in another episode they made a salad—a meat salad: no vegetables, and it included pork croutons that looked about as disgusting as they sound. The amateur chefs even made the world's largest meatball and called it the meatball Death Star. Any faint hope in human progress dies when you watch this show. Watching these guys with their so-called "Internet cooking show" reminded me of the old joke: There's nothing wrong with gluttony as long as you don't overdo it.

Naturally, we associate gluttony with food and overeating. The West, and North America in particular, appear to struggle with weight control. Statistics Canada estimates that 23 percent of Canadians are obese and US statistics suggest well over one-third of Americans are said to be obese (more women than men). I recall while living in the United Kingdom reading an obesity expert, Professor Steve Bloom at Imperial College, London say, "We are murdering ourselves with gluttony."[1]

Apparently, gluttony *really* is a "deadly sin." Gregory the Great, the one who first drew up the list of the seven deadly sins, said that gluttony occurs when we eat *too soon, too greedily, too much.* Other theologians that followed argued gluttony was deadly since it led people to mistake their stomachs for God. In other words, they worshiped food and by that act of worship, they dropped their guard and permitted other sinful and

1. Jo Willey, "Britain is murdering itself with gluttony," *Express*, September 30, 2009.

idolatrous behaviors to flourish. St. Francis of Assisi even went so far as to take ash from the fireplace and sprinkle it on his food to cut down on the enjoyment! A notable exception, however, was St. Thomas Aquinas who, having strong opinions on everything, was quite soft on gluttony, perhaps because it was well known that he had a weight problem and was described as looking a little bit like a wine barrel.

But is that really what we're talking about when we consider how the reductionism of the gospel in North America has left us "full of consumerism" yet bankrupt spiritually at the same time? I recall a conversation with a teenager many years ago in Kakuma Refugee Camp in northwestern Kenya, where he told me that when he flipped through magazines donated by kindhearted (but slightly misguided) North American Christians, the images depicting Africans always involved in extreme poverty. "What do you see when you look at North American culture in those magazines?" I asked. Without hesitating, the young Sudanese Christian responded flatly, "Spiritual poverty."

Reflecting on what has "filled us up" in our consumerist, individualistic, secularized North American context, I began to wonder more about the meaning of the sin of gluttony beyond the obvious "overeating" mantra that weight loss programs live to cure. That led me to look up the definition of gluttony, and while it is connected with excessive eating, the *Oxford Dictionary* also described it as "habitual greed." That should give one pause—*habitual greed as gluttonous behavior*. In the biblical narrative, habitual greed surfaces in the parables of Jesus. Luke recalls:

> Someone out of the crowd said, "Teacher, order my brother to give me a fair share of the family inheritance." He replied, "Mister, what makes you think it's any of my business to be a judge or mediator for you?" Speaking to the people, he went on, "Take care! Protect yourself against the least bit of greed. Life is not defined by what you have, even when you have a lot." Then he told them this story: "The farm of a certain rich man produced a terrific crop. He talked to himself: 'What can I do? My barn isn't big enough for this harvest.' Then he said, 'Here's what I'll do: I'll tear down my barns and build bigger ones. Then I'll gather in all my grain and goods, and I'll say to myself, Self, you've done well! You've got it made and can now retire. Take it easy and have the time of your life!' "Just then God showed up and said, 'Fool! Tonight you die. And your barnful

of goods—who gets it?' That's what happens when you fill your barn with Self and not with God."[2]

The background to the parable is innocent enough. A man approaches Jesus and asks him to perform a typical rabbinical role and to serve as arbitrator in a dispute something like a justice of the peace today. The problem involved an inheritance. "Tell my brother to divide the inheritance with me," the man says to Jesus.

Now wills and inheritance can be a tricky business and cause great family trouble. Just like the story of the older gentlemen who decided to splurge and get top of the line hearing aids. When he went back a month later to have them checked the technician asked, "How are they working?" "Amazing," the man responded, "I haven't heard this well in years!" "What do your children say about the new hearing aids?" inquired the technician. "Oh, I haven't told them about the new hearing aids yet but just by listening to what they've been saying I've already decided to change my will three times."

In Jesus' day, when a family inheritance was to be split, the older brother would portion out the possessions, land, and so forth, reserving a double portion for himself as the firstborn.[3] Many families did not split the inheritance but worked the land together or maintained the fishing fleet and so forth. Obviously, the younger brother here wants his inheritance but the older brother will not allow it. This will require the approval/order of a rabbi. Jesus, however, senses the selfish motives of the younger brother and refuses to rule, instead launching into the parable of the Rich Fool.

Jesus says there was a wealthy man whose farm produced an amazing crop. This good news produces, in turn, a dilemma. What to do with the abundance? There is nowhere to store his crops. Now, that's not true. He's a farmer, who has planted a crop, year after year. There *is* a place to store crops, just not the bumper crop that lies before him. He could fill his existing barns to the top, in fact to overflowing and be satisfied. But no, he says, "This is what I'll do. I will tear down my barns and build bigger ones, and there I will store all my crops. I'll say to my soul, "Soul, you've made it . . . relax, eat, drink and be merry." No sooner are the words out of the man's mouth when the voice of God thunders, "Fool! This very night your life is being demanded of you." No wonder Jesus begins by warning, "Watch

---

2. Luke 12:13–21, *The Message*.

3. Deuteronomy 21:17.

out! Be on your guard against all kinds of greed; life does not consist in an abundance of possessions."[4]

Reading the parable reminded me of Michael Frost's comments on economics and faith. Frost writes

> Now, I'm no economist, but it would seem to me that a good deal of the theoretical underpinning of free market economics is opposed by the teaching of Jesus. For example, Jesus reveals God to be a distinctively relational being, whose priority is not economic growth, but right relationships between humanity and himself and between human beings. His injunction for us to love God and our neighbor indicates his clear priority for relational wealth over financial wealth. Furthermore, his explicit teaching on the seductive nature of wealth and greed and the difficulty for the rich of gaining access to the Kingdom of God must be considered. And yet the market dictates that all growth is good, all the time. Where did the churches learn this? Not from Jesus. In fact, I have heard a stock analyst say that the market can always be trusted because it is driven by fear and greed, two qualities that orient the market to self-correct toward growth over the long term. How is putting your trust in fear and greed a reflection of the universal reign of God through Christ?[5]

Indeed, the closing line of this fear-and-greed–based parable in *The Message* leaves no ambiguity—"That's what happens when you fill your barn with Self and not with God." Walter Brueggemann identifies the presence of death at work in a culture of affluence when he writes, "For people in our culture and in our churches, death operates in the seductive power of consumer economics with its engines of greed; in the mesmerizing of military power and its production of fear, insecurity, anxiety, brutality, and a craving for vengeance; in the reduction of all life, human and nonhuman, to a bartering of commodities, until we and our neighbors are all perceived as means and not as ends."[6] This is the rub of reductionism that encourages gluttony as habitual greed. For many, even if they hold "membership" in a church, live for themselves and not for the glory of God. A culture of affluence, rooted in the religion of consumerism, leads to an outward form of "window dressing Christianity" but sadly results in a de facto state of "Christian Functional Atheism." Christian Functional Atheism (CFA) is

4. Luke 12:14, *NIV.*

5. Frost, *Road to Missional,* 72–73.

6. Brueggemann, *Biblical Perspectives on Evangelism,* 40.

when people believe they are Christian based on their financial gifts to the church or their regular (or occasional) attendance in church but who live as if there is no God. The de facto state of their spirituality is that they are most comfortable with their own individual self as the center of the universe. Found in the church today, CFA sometimes appears cloaked in clerical vestments or hiding behind lay members good works, but it is a reality of those who shun obedience to Christ in favor of a lifestyle that is "without God." Those who propagate this myth of Christian Functional Atheism are appearing more frequently on the media's radar screen.

A recent article in *The Economist* explored this phenomenon by asking how modern denominations are responding, in particular, to clergy who openly renounce any belief in God. Tracing the movement of Christian leaders towards a position of public atheism, the article moves from John Robinson's 1963 book *Honest to God* that shook the Church of England, to a Danish Lutheran Priest named Thorkild Grosboll who denied God's existence and Christ's resurrection but managed to keep his leadership position until retirement, to the United Church of Canada's Minister Gretta Vosper who is an avowed atheist dedicated to the eradication of religion. Visiting one of Vosper's "services" *The Economist* reported:

> At her most recent Sunday service, she preached a sermon about her great passion for the church. Instead of the traditional "Amen," the congregation responded with a cry of "in this, our time of need, may love abound" then sang a hymn that made no mention of God. As Ms. Vosper explained afterwards: "I removed the language that reinforces moral authority. We should instead of using the word *God* use the words that mean what we mean, calling for justice, a need for compassion."[7]

Missional leadership in a culture of affluence appears all the more difficult if leaders within the church are comfortable publically naming their Christian Functional Atheism and promoting themselves above God's sovereignty and obedience to Christ. Surely we are witnessing the ultimate *reductionism*—the recasting of the story between God and humankind where God's control and authority is now exclusively in human hands. This retro garden of Eden "gone wrong" narrative continues to haunt humanity to this day.

---

7. "Clergy, Heresy and Atheism—the Limits of Liberalism," *The Economist,* June 15, 2015, www.economist.com/blogs/erasmus/2015/06/faith-heresy-and-atheism-0.

It's time to look again at the parable of the Rich Fool. This story not only unsettles our consumerist values of security and pleasure, but it also attacks our sinful reductionist take on the gospel that enables Christian Functional Atheism to flourish in the church today. The Rich Fool, found both in the Gospel of Luke and the Gospel of Thomas (Tommy boy did not make the final cut of the Biblical canon), is worth a closer look. The character is blessed with abundance. I don't see any judgment on that but wait for God's judgment on what comes next. Remember, the definition of gluttony that we are working with is *habitual greed*. The man plants crops every year and when the harvest comes he is in the rhythm of deciding what to do with the richness of the crops. John Wesley's approach to wealth is often cited—earn all you can, save all you can, give all you can.[8] Well, this gentleman excels at the first two but not the third.

It never occurs to him that he could fill his barns to the max and then give away the surplus. He has already been blessed beyond measure but instead of *generosity* he chooses the path of *gluttony* or habitual greed. The soliloquy betrays where his heart really lies: *my* crops, *my* barns, *my* grain, *my* goods, and *my* soul. No wonder God calls him a fool. Even if he has an outward look of religiosity the reference to *my* soul betrays his Christian Functional Atheism, which appears to put him in control of his own soul.

Parables, of course, are meant to unsettle us. In fact, a rule of thumb might be if you read a parable and you are not uncomfortable, go back and read it again—you've missed something. For as challenging as this parable appears at first glance, the most powerful statement comes at the end of Jesus' lesson, "So it is with those who store up treasures for themselves but are not rich towards God." *Rich towards God.* What if leadership in a culture of affluence is about witnessing to a life that is "rich toward God" rather than one directed at self and poorly masked with Christian Functional Atheism? What if missional leadership could witness to the power of the gospel by demonstrating lives transformed from habitual greed to habitual generosity? What if lukewarm Laodicean Christianity could bubble with Pentecostal fire? What if local mission communities could be known as places where God's Spirit was helping people habitually choose salvation over security, purpose over pleasure, generosity over gluttony? It's time to

8. Wesley's threefold mantra regarding wealth was to combat the sin of sloth (earn all you can), pride (save all you can and don't spend on foolish things), and greed (give all you can).

stop pulling weeds and instead plant seeds. To this great missional task we must now turn.

God expects nothing less.
Christ asks nothing more.
May the Spirit make it so.

Part II

Leaving Laodicea Behind

"Then I heard the voice of the Lord saying,
'Whom shall I send? And who will go for us?'
And I said, Here am I. Send me!"

—Isaiah 6:8

"The church participates in God's mission in the world because it can do no
other; it was created for this purpose. This purpose is encoded within the very
make-up of the nature of the church: it is missionary by nature."

—Craig Van Gelder, *The Missional Church and Denominations*

Chapter Six

Fifty Shades of Grace—Lessons from Jonah
(Call, Confusion, Confession, Conversion, Community)

For you, O Lord, are good and forgiving,
abounding in steadfast love to all who call on your name.

—Psalm 86: 5

M y first church after ordination was in Northern Ontario in a pulp
and paper mill town called Dryden. In that little town, miles from
anywhere surrounded by rocks and trees and lakes, live some of the loveli-
est people you will ever find. It doesn't take a newcomer long to discover
that on the weekends a good number of the men in town disappear to go
hunting or fishing with their buddies. In order to connect with the guys in
the church a pastor has to pick up either a fishing rod or a hunting rifle—I
opted for the rod and the lure. Fishing boats are a great place for pastoral
conversations. You find yourself in a small group, on the water, with hours
of waiting and time to reflect on life in the beauty of God's creation. Oh
sure, there's always a bit of storytelling about "the one that got away" and a
few tall tales shared but there is also a considerable amount of discussion
on God, humanity, and what's right and wrong with the world.

One afternoon, after a long Saturday of fishing, I dropped a man from our church off at home and his wife came out to say hello. Being her pastor as well, I said, "I feel bad taking your husband away all day like this—I hope you don't mind." "Mind?" she smiled broadly, "oh, I don't mind. After all, you know the old wisdom saying, 'Give a man a fish and he will eat for the day. Teach a man to fish *and I get this whole house to myself for the weekend!* It's perfect!"

When you read through the Bible and come across the story of Jonah in the First Testament it's not hard to see that we are given one of the Bible's best "tall tales." One might even be tempted to say it's a "whale of a tale." For people who participate in a Christian community that adheres to the Revised Common Lectionary, you can be in church all your life and never hear the Jonah and the whale story. There's a more palatable snippet about Jonah and Nineveh in one place in the lectionary that is less offensive to more modernist-minded folks who have trouble explaining people inside whales to their witty friends at cocktail parties. But it is important to hear the Jonah story in its entirety if it is to help us find our way out of our "Laodicean captivity." We need to begin with the call to Jonah, a prophet, mentioned in 2 Kings. The call from God is to go to Nineveh, that great city, and prophesy against their wickedness. The book of Jonah begins:

> One day long ago, God's Word came to Jonah, Amittai's son: "Up on your feet and on your way to the big city of Nineveh! Preach to them. They're in a bad way and I can't ignore it any longer.[1]

Our way home begins with God's call. But watch what happens next. Jonah hears the call of God and decides to go the other way.

> But Jonah got up and went the other direction to Tarshish, running away from God. He went down to the port of Joppa and found a ship headed for Tarshish. He paid the fare and went on board, joining those going to Tarshish—as far away from God as he could get.[2]

Jonah acts a little bit like a substitute teacher who gets a text at 6 AM on her mobile device and has to decide whether to take the assignment for the day or roll over and keep sleeping. Jonah rolls over. Why? He's confused.

Nineveh, that "great" gentile city, located across the riverbank from the modern Mosul in Iraq, was part of the Assyrian Empire in Jonah's day—and

1. Jonah 1:1–2, *The Message.*
2. Jonah 1:3, *The Message.*

it was the enemy. In fact, in 722 BC the Assyrians roll into the northern kingdom of Israel. They conquer the local inhabitants, intermarry, and—voila—we get the Samaritans of the New Testament. God's call confuses Jonah.

"No thanks," Jonah says and he decides to get as far away from cell reception as possible, heads south, and jumps aboard a ship in the ancient port of Joppa, today a suburb of the modern city of Tel Aviv. This is the same place where one day Peter will see his vision at Simon the tanner's house, have a change of heart about the Gentiles, and head off to chat with Cornelius the centurion, revealing just how inclusive the kingdom of God is in the eyes of the Father, Son, and Holy Spirit. Jonah is about to learn his own lesson of God's inclusivity with the Gentiles but first, in his confused state, he jumps on a ship heading the opposite direction from God's call.

Jonah isn't the only person confused when it comes to God's call and what mission means in the world. While mission and evangelism are often used as synonyms in the church, there is value in making a distinction between the two concepts. Mission, according to David Bosch, is the wider of the two terms and involves the

> total task that God has set the church for the salvation of the world. In its missionary involvement, the church steps out of itself, into the wider world. It crosses all kinds of frontiers and barriers: geographical, social, political, ethnic, cultural, religious, ideological. Into all these areas the church-in-mission carries the message of God's salvation. Ultimately, then, mission means being involved in the redemption of the universe and the glorification of God.[3]

Too often mission is seen only as a department of the church with a focus on how to grow and support the numerical and financial well-being of the institution. Michael Frost argues that mission is primarily concerned with the reign and rule of God the Trinity:

> The practice and attitude of mission is rooted in a belief in the kingship of the Triune God. God reigns even if not one soul on the face of the earth acknowledges it. His reign is full and complete, an eternal and non-negotiable reality, not enlarged nor diminished by the number of people who believe it and yield to it. Our mission, then, is to alert people to this irrefutable reality, by both announcement and demonstration.[4]

3. Quoted in Chilcote, ed., *Study of Evangelism*, 9.
4. Frost, *Road to Missional*, 25.

If we approach mission as the church's partnership with the sovereign God in the redemption of the whole world through the victory of empty cradle, cross, and grave, then we need to be clear as well about the more narrow definition of evangelism.

In making a distinction between mission and evangelism David Bosch contends that evangelism is that dimension and activity of the church's mission that seeks to offer every person everywhere a valid opportunity to be directly challenged by the gospel of explicit faith in Jesus Christ, with a view to embracing him as savior, becoming a living member of his community, and being enlisted in his service of reconciliation, peace, and justice on earth.[5] To help us better understand what this ministry of evangelism looks like Robert Webber suggests three key marks of evangelism: "Evangelism is a process. Evangelism takes place over a period of time. Evangelism brings new believers to spiritual maturity."[6] While I agree with his insights, I believe Webber is missing a fourth crucial aspect of evangelism—the role of the Christian community. It is primarily within the work and witness of local mission communities that people are nurtured through evangelism into a lasting relationship with, and discipleship to, Jesus Christ. It is the local congregation that provides opportunities for people to, in time, become evangelists themselves on behalf of the community of faith. Retired Canadian senator and former head of the World Council of Churches Dr. Lois Wilson once told someone who was inquiring about Christianity, "I can tell you a few things but the best thing you can do is find a good church and figure it out there."

In addition, as we struggle to define evangelism within the broader mission of the church we must not lose sight of in whose name and by whose power our common ministry is exercised. Too often evangelism can be narrowly defined as a neat and tidy human-initiated "to do list" for congregational recovery without recognizing that the church relies solely on the inspiration and power of the Holy Spirit in this evangelizing work and, indeed, all of its various ministries. Evangelism is first and foremost our Triune God's idea.[7] While we share the same conviction today of Christ's

---

5. Bosch, *Evangelism*, 17.

6. Webber, *Ancient Future Evangelism*, 13.

7. In the Reformed tradition, this understanding of God as the primary agent of conversion through evangelism is deeply rooted. The Westminster Confession of Faith 1646, Article XXV *Of the Church*, III, states, "Unto this catholic and visible Church, Christ hath given the ministry, oracles, and ordinances of God, for the gathering and perfecting of the saints, in this life, to the end of the world; and doth by his own presence and Spirit,

presence in the church and work through the Spirit as our Reformed ancestors, Stuart Murray reminds us that followers of Calvin and Luther were deeply embedded in Christendom and, working with the assumption that Europe was already Christian, focused their mission on the Catholic Church's "serious doctrinal errors and gross moral corruption" instead of evangelism, believing that evangelists were obsolete.[8] Murray argues that it was the Anabaptists who believed that Jesus' command in Matthew 28 to "Go therefore and make disciples of all nations baptizing them in the name of the Father, and of the Son, and of the Holy Spirit . . ." had not yet been fulfilled in Europe, so evangelism was vital as a result.[9] While we live and minister in a post-Christendom context today, too often we echo our Reformed ancestors' assumptions that when it comes to the gifts Christ offers his church in Ephesians 4. We too often value prophets, pastors, and teachers in mainline congregations over apostles and evangelists.[10] By locating our evangelism in the heart of local mission communities, we seek to claim back the gifts of evangelism that Christ has bestowed upon his body in the world we call the church so we may reach "the full stature of Christ."

Therefore, a helpful working definition of evangelism would be *a congregational life that helps people witness to their trust in Jesus, and by the Spirit's power, transforms them within community into disciples of Christ who participate in God's saving mission for the world.* Evangelistic preaching, in turn, is a dedication and commitment on the part of the preacher to use the homiletical action within worship to help people place their trust in Jesus and empower and enable them, through the Holy Spirit, to become evangelists themselves in the places where they live, work, and play.

Mission and evangelism are at the heart of missional leadership. Stuart Murray writes, "Missiologists have increasingly been drawn to the Latin phrase *Missio Dei* to express the conviction that mission is not the invention, responsibility or programme of human beings (per se), but flows from the character and purpose of God."[11] Missional theology begins with the assumption that the church does not have a mission, but rather *God's Mission has a church.* Missional practice hears and responds to Christ's command in John 20, "Peace be with you! As the Father has sent me, I am sending

---

according to his promise, make them effectual."

8. Murray, *Church Planting,* 95.

9. Ibid., 96.

10. Ephesians 4:11–14.

11. Murray, *Church Planting,* 95.

you." While popular "missional" language encourages Christians to move beyond the safety of stained glass sanctuaries in order to "join God in the neighborhood," it does not devalue the importance of local congregations. In fact, missional practice is quite the opposite. As Ross Hastings at Regent College notes, "the missional church (is) the church that participates in the love and life of the triune God, as a continuance of the mission of the Son from the Father, by the Spirit."[12] In many ways, missional church is a beautiful reimaging of our ecclesiology in light of a robust missiology, rooted in God's sovereign activity in the world. Missional theology takes seriously, in equal parts, the Triune God's gathering, upbuilding, and sending of disciples into the world. Mission, therefore, is not a subcommittee of the Session nor is it something that a department of the wider church does in impoverished neighborhoods or foreign countries. Instead missional theology "flips the script" on our understanding of what it means to be a redeemed Christ follower in this world and reshapes both Christian community and leadership as a result.

Knowing more fully now the missional nature of God, as well as God's desire to partner with sinful humanity in the world of reconciling the world, it will come as no surprise when we return to the story of Jonah and discover that apparently you can't outrun the Almighty. A storm blows up, or as the King James Version so politely says, "a tempest," but this is no tempest in a teapot. No, the sailors start praying to any and every "small g god" they can think of and nothing helps. It's a little bit like returning to that great "philosopher" Ricky Bobby who, when he thinks his underwear is on fire in the movie *Talladega Nights*, calls out to every deity he can remember until finally settling on invoking the name of Tom Cruise for help!

With their deity laundry list exhausted, the sailors suddenly realize their passenger is fast asleep in the ship while the storm rages. Hmm, that reminds me of another Bible story where someone is fast asleep during a storm at sea. They wake Jonah and he confesses that, "I am a Hebrew. I worship the Lord, the God of heaven who made the sea and the dry land." Now the sailors know they are in big trouble. Jonah looks like those guys after Dog the Bounty Hunter catches them and they are waiting to go to prison—dejected and resigned to their fate. The sailors take Jonah up on his offer of tossing him over the side and into the sea and the storm is stilled.

That's when the big fish shows up. Apparently it's not necessarily a whale. Call. Confusion. And now what? The Bible says God sent a big fish

---

12. Hastings, *Missional God, Missional Church*, 16.

to swallow Jonah and while in the belly of the beast he has a good think and a prayer. The book of Jonah describes it like this:

> Then Jonah prayed to his God from the belly of the fish.
> He prayed:
> "In trouble, deep trouble, I prayed to God.
>   He answered me.
> From the belly of the grave I cried, 'Help!'
>   You heard my cry.
> You threw me into ocean's depths,
>   into a watery grave,
> With ocean waves, ocean breakers
>   crashing over me.
> I said, 'I've been thrown away,
>   thrown out, out of your sight.
> I'll never again lay eyes
>   on your Holy Temple.'
> Ocean gripped me by the throat.
>   The ancient Abyss grabbed me and held tight.
> My head was all tangled in seaweed
>   at the bottom of the sea where the mountains take root.
> I was as far down as a body can go,
>   and the gates were slamming shut behind me forever—
> Yet you pulled me up from that grave alive,
>   O God, my God!
> When my life was slipping away,
>   I remembered God,
> And my prayer got through to you,
>   made it all the way to your Holy Temple.
> Those who worship hollow gods, god-frauds,
>   walk away from their only true love.
> But I'm worshiping you, God,
>   calling out in thanksgiving!
> And I'll do what I promised I'd do!
>   Salvation belongs to God!"[13]

Form criticism folks could help us tease out what we're actually seeing in this prayer in the midst of the story. But what is clear is that God's call has put Jonah into confusion that now leads to *confession and conversion*. Call. Confusion. Confession. Conversion. As missional leaders in a culture of affluence, conversion is a critical movement initiated by God. As Walter Brueggemann describes ministry to future generations, "Insofar as our

13. Jonah 2:1–10, *The Message*.

young are practitioners of secular indifference, or adherents to legalistic individualism, they are candidates for an evangelical conversion."[14] A young man named Jonah would agree. The story continues with the big fish then "spitting" Jonah out onto the beach, although the actual Hebrew word is closer to vomit. And after a shower and a stiff drink the Bible says . . . the word of the Lord came to Jonah—*a second time.*

This time Jonah goes to Nineveh and it turns out to be a big place. It's a three-day walk across and Jonah must have wondered what little effect his prophetic call would have on this massive enemy city. Like a farm kid in the big city for the first time he wanders around looking at the big buildings and all the people. Then he follows through on his calling—announcing in a hoarse and reluctant voice, "Forty more days and Nineveh will be overthrown."

And something strange happens. People pay attention. Word spreads. God's call leads to confusion. People are puzzled and intrigued by this message. The city is suddenly abuzz with this call but uncertain of what to do next. The confusion ends when the call of God reaches the king's ears. He knows this prophet of Yahweh means business. The king responds to the call and confusion with confession and conversion. The entire city is ordered to repent in the hopes that confession and conversion might save them yet. The city puts on sackcloth and ashes. Heck, even the cows are covered in sackcloth and ashes. It's not every day that you see cattle repent. Call. Confusion. Confession. Conversion. *And* (new) community. Nineveh is a changed community.

God calls Jonah not to be just any kind of leader but a missional leader. Our world and Christ's church desperately needs missional leaders like Jonah today. As Allan Roxburgh notes, "We need leaders who can read our situation from a specific perspective: God is the primary agent in our world."[15] Roxburgh pushes his argument further by stating

> The unraveling of the churches and the transformation of society are not only the result of socio-cultural shifts. First and foremost, they are the actions of God. We need leaders able to perceive the shape of God's activities in the midst of a great unraveling. The "disembedding" of Christian life in our society is the work of God. There is no putting back together the religious consensus that once had the church near the center. God's Spirit is up to something

14. Brueggemann, *Biblical Perspectives on Evangelism*, 97.

15. Bowen, ed., *Green Shoots Out of Dry Ground*, 186.

massively disruptive across Western societies. Perhaps the Spirit is pushing the churches into spaces they cannot manage or control so that they might rediscover their missional identity. The implication, if accepted, is that we are looking at the re-founding, rather than the renewing, of the church. The socio-cultural milieu in which most of our churches were formed no longer exists. The shapers of the churches in the West were often wise leaders and brilliant missiologists. But in the modern period, churches and their leaders became chaplains to nation states, social contracts and individualism. We are past the point of renewing church life around these assumptions. Our vocation as leaders is to re-found churches as missionary communities of the kingdom.[16]

Jonah, of course, did not understand himself to be a missional leader partnering with God in mission. No, in fact, even when God's redemptive mission bears fruit Jonah misses the point. Jonah thinks that God's compassion is not fair. After all that Jonah has been through (still smelling like a bad shrimp cocktail) the least God could do was a little "smiting and smoting." The book of Jonah records his rant:

> Jonah was furious. He lost his temper. He yelled at God, "God! I knew it—when I was back home, I knew this was going to happen! That's why I ran off to Tarshish! I knew you were sheer grace and mercy, not easily angered, rich in love, and ready at the drop of a hat to turn your plans of punishment into a program of forgiveness!"[17]

Whenever I hear Jonah's response I always think of moments in pastoral ministry when people bring the same complaint about life, about God, about everything. It's like when the hardworking member of the church sits defeated in the pew and tells you about the latest job interview where the position when to someone else. It's not fair. Or when the couple whose marriage is in tatters sits and talks about all the dreams they once had that are over. It's not fair. Or when you sit in the living room sipping bitter coffee speaking with members of your church whose teenager was killed by a drunk driver who is now out on parole. It's not fair. Or when the irresponsible brother overshadows the dutiful daughter at the last minute by flying in for a quick eulogy while having left others to the hard work of palliative

16. Ibid., 186.

17. Jonah 4:1–2, *The Message*.

care and probate. It's not fair. But this story is not about human fairness. It's about the grace and the mercy of God. Jonah even said it himself.

It's a story about how God can and does take sinful, ordinary, broken people like you and me, and acts out God's sovereign will through us. It's about God's invitation to people who have lost their way whether it be ancient Ninevites or contemporary "Laodicean captives" in North America to hear God's call, struggle through the confusion, make confession that comes clean with the past, experience conversion and live in a whole new community that as Christians we know as the church. Darrell Guder argues that "the story of Jonah, one of the few Old Testament episodes which appear to be missionary in nature, actually addresses God's summons to Israel to be a compassionate witness even over against such unworthy subjects as the Ninevites."[18] Jonah's story reminds me of Peter Rollins's claim that, "once we acknowledge that we are *becoming* Christian, *becoming* Church and *being* saved, then the other can be seen as a possible instrument of our further conversion. Even a brief reflection upon the darkness in our own lives bears testimony to the fact that we need to be evangelized as much, if not more, than those around us."[19] Jonah's problem is ours today as well. Jonah is a "'missionary' without a missionary's heart."[20] Thank God (literally) that the Holy Spirit is turning up the heat on our polite, socially respectable, lukewarm Laodicean Christianity. The need to re-evangelize a post-Constantinian North American culture of affluence reminds us how much we need Nineveh to see what God can and will do by grace.

Every Christian community in North America, large or small, rural, urban, or suburban, has the potential to be the kind of place where contemporary Jonahs stand and announce God's call, that leads people in confusion to look at their lives, drives them to their knees in confession, helps them testify to conversion in order to enjoy the newness of life in the community we call the church. Right now in your community there is someone you know who has finally given up on the empty marketing guru's promise of forty days to a "new you," how to lose weight fast, or how to get rich even faster. No more. They are ready to hear God's call. There are other people in your community also waiting for that call. Forty days until they hear back about the job interview. They're in Nineveh. Forty days until the bank takes back the house. They're in Nineveh. Forty days until the court

18. Guder, *Continuing Conversion*, 33.

19. Rollins, *Speak of God*, 5–6.

20. Guder, *Continuing Conversion*, 33.

decides who gets the kids. They're in Nineveh. Forty days until they can see the specialist and figure out whether they live or die. They're in Nineveh.

Pray to God that there is someone beside them who can speak with love about the other One who once slept in a boat through a stormy night and who stands ready to declare "Peace be still!" that leads us to wonder in confusion, "who is it that the even the winds and the waves obey?"[21]

Call. Confusion. Confession. Conversion. Community.
God invites us to take our first steps on the path full of grace and mercy that leads away from our Laodicean captivity. The journey begins by acknowledging that:

> Whether one is answering God's call this day or running in the opposite direction.
>
>> God's grace will find us.
>
> Whether one is praying for his/her neighbor or thinking ill of those around.
>
>> God's love can transform us.
>
> Whether one is preaching on a soapbox or on their knees in confession.
>
>> God's peace and mercy surround us.
>
> God will never give up on us . . . even if we think we're the one that got away.

---

21. Matthew 8:27, *NIV.*

Chapter Seven

Q3 Minority Report
Following Jesus in the Ruins of Christendom

"If you don't know where you're going, you might end up someplace else."

—Yogi Berra

The birthday party invitation sat on the kitchen table awaiting an answer. The little grade two girl had invited all her classmates to a party, and our family was the only hold-out. The birthday party was scheduled for Sunday morning at 10 AM. Ugh. Church hour. To top it all off—the little girl celebrating the birthday was named "Faith." Lovely. Ironic. And so it has come to this.

When we imagine our way forward out of the Laodicean ruins of Christendom in North America, it will involve a whole new way of living the gospel. It requires a great attentiveness to catechesis for all ages and a starting place of acceptance that we are sharing faith from a minority perspective and not the dominant leader of spiritual thought. For example, when my wife and I were chewing over the birthday party invitation from "Faith" scheduled for Sunday morning, we realized that not once had we ever stopped to wonder whether our usual Saturday birthday party invitations could have caused a problem for Jewish friends keeping Shabbat. In fact, we have a lot to learn from friends who have practiced and kept the faith as a minority.

Michael Frost acknowledges that our newfound place (or lack thereof) in a post-Christendom world means that our mission and ministry will look radically different than earlier generations. Frost states,

> When we have no impressive buildings and no swollen budgets to sustain our work, often only then do we realize that the best we have to offer this post-Christendom world is the quality of our relationships, the power of our trustworthiness, and the wonder of our generosity. . . . Is it too simplistic to say that we earn that right [to be heard] through our authentic lifestyles? In a culture yearning for authenticity—the real—the pressure is on us in the Christian community now more than ever to put our time and money where our mouth is and live what we preach.[1]

Missional leadership in a post-Christendom context must take seriously the need to form disciples in a culture of affluence that seeks to undermine the loyalty that Christ demands. Jessica Duckworth has provided an excellent glimpse into the Evangelical Lutheran Church in America's attempt to take newcomers (or pre-Christians) seriously and to help them take steps towards faith in Jesus. In *Wide Welcome: How the Unsettling Presence of Newcomers Can Save the Church*, Duckworth names the "deliberate disestablishment" required for mainline Protestant congregations and leaders to become the church of the cross so that, "the ecclesia crucis beckons irresistibly to be sculpted and carved, reshaped and repacked by young and old, newcomer and established member together."[2]

Catechesis is essential in a post-Christendom culture where the dominant culture no longer transmits the gospel (or a distorted version of it) through mass media and public institutions. The responsibility of making disciples has been returned (properly!) to the church. To notice, name, and nurture God's call to discipleship for those within the Christian community, newcomer and established member alike become a critical part of the church's mission today.[3] Discipleship, Jessica Duckworth reminds us, is not

1. Frost, *Exiles*, 99.

2. Duckworth, *Wide Welcome*, 2.

3. I'm borrowing the language of the Forum for Theological Education here. FTE's long-standing commitment to helping to nurture and support young adults' call to ministry is a wonderful witness to the gospel in North America. As a member of FTE's Board of Trustees, I am privileged to see firsthand the amazing ways that the Holy Spirit

innate, as we are clearly not born disciples of the risen Christ. Duckworth argues:

> Discipleship is experienced and learned, we become disciples of Jesus Christ. Thus, attention to learning or catechesis is necessary within the church. Discipleship and faith are interrelated, mutually informing one another. Discipleship and faith are also distinct. Discipleship is learning through participation in Christian practices, gaining knowledge and skills to sustain a Christian identity. To be clear, faith is not learned. Faith cannot be reduced to knowledge or skill. Faith is a gift of the Holy Spirit. Faith enables and sustains the life of disciples within and beyond the ecclesia crucis.[4]

While the next chapter looks more closely at the Christian practices I use to help make missionary disciples in a post-Christendom context, this chapter explores a basic foundation required for those practices to take deep root. As I pastored in and amongst a culture of affluence that include a large number of atheists or members of the church's "Alumni Association" it became clear that people needed to address head on three critical questions that I've come to call Q3. Q3—or three questions that will change your life—are basic building blocks of discipleship that help inform the practices that follow in the next chapter.

Q3—PART ONE: WHO AM I?

"We are what we believe in."

—C. S. Lewis

From the moment of our birth we are assigned a certain identity. Some of us spend a good portion of our lives running away from that identity and others embrace it. Depending on our family's background we receive our physical features, race, initial language, and culture. From our family's socioeconomic standing we begin life at a certain place and geographic

---

is working through the organization helping churches raise up the next generation of disciples.

4. Duckworth, *Wide Welcome*, 3.

location. We inherit spirituality and moral values of one kind or another including, for some, atheism and consumerism in this late stage capitalism of the Western world. From our beginnings we are offered a basic map and compass that marks the pathways and boundaries by which we *should* make our way in the world.

For some of us, our families of origin are a source of great blessing and strength. For others, they are a place of deep hurt and disillusionment. For all of us, however, the answer to the question "Who am I?" comes "preloaded" in a basic way from our social location and family of origin. But, just like a new iPhone that has a basic setup at the time of purchase, by the time you leave the Apple store you are already deleting and adding new features, apps, and contacts that make it your own.

As individuals walking a pilgrimage through this world we must carefully unlearn the identities that we were given in early childhood.[5] This is particularly tricky when the unlearning takes place not in a static or controlled environment, but one that is constantly shifting amid influences of the surrounding culture.

James van der Walt from Pretoria, South Africa offered a compelling example of this in a Ted Talk. He reminded the audience that scientific study has proven that every seven years or so we have a totally new body.[6] Not only cells are replaced but also human creatures by adulthood do not have a single atom from their original childhood body. He pushed the argument further to suggest that even memories change over time as we put different life experiences into perspective. The event itself did not change but how we relate and remember it has changed. Our self-perception is an evolving notion that is influenced, in part, by how others see us and express it in words and actions.

For many, as we move into adulthood "who we are" is synonymous with "what we do." In other words, one might identify themselves as a mother, an accountant, and a marathon runner. Or one might lean towards answering the question "Who am I?" in terms of being a single/partnered, urban/suburban, hipster/Lululemon wearing, rock climbing/soccer playing, vegetarian/steak loving, Canucks/Maple Leafs fan and so forth. The response to "Who am I?" is a careful deconstruction/reconstruction of our

5. Readers will recognize in Q3 a nod to philosopher Paul Ricour's first naivete through critical reflection to second naivete. The question of "Who am I?" involves an acceptance of our "pre-loaded" identity but an encounter with the risen Christ leads us to reflection to the reconstruction of our identity in second naivete as "Who am I in Jesus?"

6. James van der Walt, *Ted Talk: Who Am I?*, October 2011, www.ted.com.

own identity based on what we value, who we share life with, and how we spend our time and money. But surely, we are more than the work we do or the hobbies we enjoy or the company we keep.

I suppose there is also the question of whether or not we should trust the self-image that we have created and project to others on a daily basis. The Christian tradition has always been very up front about our ability to deceive both others and ourselves. The book of Genesis tells us a story of creation in which God calls everything, including human creatures, good. But we also hear a story of the fall, a sad tale of the freedom of human creatures run amok that ends in a state of sin—which is brokenness and alienation—separation from God and other human creatures. The Apostle Paul describes living with the reality of sin:

> What I don't understand about myself is that I decide one way, but then I act another, doing things I absolutely despise. So if I can't be trusted to figure out what is best for myself and then do it, it becomes obvious that God's command is necessary. But I need something more! For if I know the law but still can't keep it, and if the power of sin within me keeps sabotaging my best intentions, I obviously need help! I realize that I don't have what it takes. I can will it, but I can't do it. I decide to do good, but I don't really do it; I decide not to do bad, but then I do it anyway. My decisions, such as they are, don't result in actions. Something has gone wrong deep within me and gets the better of me every time.[7]

Does that sound familiar? It's a little bit like watching those Dove soap commercials online known as the "Dove Real Beauty Sketch."[8] Dove invited several women to come to a brightly lit studio and have their image sketched by an artist who did *not* see the women but, sitting behind a curtain, instead had the women describe themselves to the artist. After the women left one by one, another group of women who were planted in the waiting room were called in to describe the same people on the basis of how *they* observed the women. Well, you can imagine the result. The two images were very, very different. The sketches of the women as described by their own observation were sad and highlighted features they were not proud of. The sketches (of the same women!) as described by a casual observer were beautiful and life-giving. How we perceive ourselves, and the world around us, through the lens of a fallen world is often *not* to be trusted.

7. Romans 7:15–20, *The Message.*
8. www.realbeautysketches.dove.ca.

An often-quoted line from the Greek philosopher Socrates is, "The unexamined life is not worth living." In some ways, it's a harsh saying. Socrates did not say, "The unexamined life is less meaningful but still a gift." No, his thoughts still challenge us today. If we float through life without digging deep into the question, "Who am I?" we could miss the whole purpose of what it means to be "human beings being human." Legendary African American preacher Howard Thurman has captured this calling so beautifully in his work, "The Sound of the Genuine." Thurman invites us to drill down to the core of what it means to be human when he writes:

> There is in every person something that waits and listens for the sound of the genuine in herself [or himself] . . . There is in you something that waits and listens for the sound of the genuine in yourself. Nobody like you has ever been born and no one like you will ever be born again—you are the only one.

> If you cannot hear the sound of the genuine within you, you will never find whatever it is for which you are searching and if you hear it and then do not follow it, it was better that you had never been born. You are the only you that has ever lived; your idiom is the only idiom of its kind in all the existences, and if you cannot hear the sound of the genuine in you, you will all of your life spend your days on the ends of strings that somebody else pulls.

> So the burden of what I have to say to you is, "What is your name—who are you—and can you find a way to hear the sound of the genuine in yourself?" There are so many [voices and] noises going on inside of you, so many echoes of all sorts, so many internalizing of the rumble and the traffic going on in your minds, the confusions, the disorders by which your environment is peopled that I wonder if you can get still enough—not quiet enough—still enough to hear rumbling up from your unique and essential idiom the sound of the genuine in you. I don't know if you can. But this is your assignment.

> The sound of the genuine is flowing through you. Don't be deceived and thrown off by all the noises that are a part even of your dreams [and] your ambitions that you don't hear the sound of the genuine in you. Because that is the only true guide you will ever have and if you don't have that you don't have a thing. Cultivate the discipline of listening to the sound of the genuine in yourself.[9]

9. Thurman, "Sound of the Genuine."

Part II: Leaving Laodicea Behind

Last century there was a Christian pastor named Dietrich Bonhoeffer who lived in Germany during the disturbing rise of the Nazi regime. While large numbers of people, including Christians, were swept up in the Nazi propaganda, Bonhoeffer used the tools of the Christian tradition—Scripture, prayer, reason, church history, discernment, and the revelation of the Holy Spirit—to arrive at a very different and dangerous conclusion. The world view that the Nazi regime was developing was evil and had to be stopped. Bonhoeffer separated from other Christians who were endorsing Hitler's ways and secretly supported the resistance movement. He helped establish a rival "confessing church" and set up an independent seminary in Finkenwalde, Germany. Bonhoeffer is best remembered by many, however, for this role in the failed plot to blow up Hitler. Dietrich Bonhoeffer was put in prison where he eventually met his end on April 9, 1945 at Flossenburg Concentration Camp. His letters from prison were later published and have served as a rich source of spiritual reflection on what it means to be a human being, being human. He includes in his letters from prison a poem simply entitled, "Who am I?" Bonhoeffer writes just one month before his execution:

> Who am I?
> *They often tell me I would step from my cell's confinement calmly, cheerfully, firmly, like a squire from his country-house.*
>
> Who am I?
> *They often tell me I would talk to my warden freely and friendly and clearly, as though it were mine to command.*
>
> Who am I?
> *They also tell me I would bear the days of misfortune equably, smilingly, proudly, like one accustomed to win. Am I then really all that which other men tell of, or am I only what I know of myself, restless and longing and sick, like a bird in a cage, struggling for breath, as though hands were compressing my throat, yearning for colors, for flowers, for the voices of birds, thirsting for words of kindness, for neighborliness, trembling with anger at despotisms and petty humiliation, tossing in expectation of great events, powerlessly trembling for friends at an infinite distance, weary and empty at praying, at thinking, at making, faint and ready to say farewell to it all.*
>
> Who am I?
> *This or the other? Am I one person today, and tomorrow another? Am I both at once? A hypocrite before others, and before myself a*

contemptibly woebegone weakling? Or is something within me still
like a beaten army, fleeing in disorder from victory already achieved?

Who am I?
They mock me, these lonely questions of mine.
Whoever I am, Thou knowest, O God, I am thine.[10]

Dietrich Bonhoeffer's brutally honest words offer us insight into our common human dilemma regarding identity. First, there is the question of how
others see us. This consumes so much of our time and worry. Will others
accept us? Judge us? Love us? Hurt us? Accept us? Abandon us? Second,
how do we see ourselves? Is there a major disconnect between how the
world sees us and/or the image we seek to project verses how we actually
see ourselves? In our heart, how do we see ourselves and might there be
a way to understand who we are by acknowledging *whose we are?* Third,
there is the too easily forgotten question of how God sees us.

I recall standing a few years ago at our local NorthShore hospital in
blue scrubs and feeling more than a little out of place. While my wife Laura
was being prepped to deliver our third child by C-section, I was told by a
surly nurse to "put these scrubs on and stay out of the way." I dutifully put
on the generic "Coastal Health" scrubs and was left in a waiting area until
the moment when dads are permitted in the surgical suite. Left with nothing else to do, and being a sign of the times, I did what any self-respecting
person of my generation would do—I went on Facebook. I posted a cryptic
message that was a statement about the little life that we were anticipat-
ing any moment—a statement about all of life and our identity as human
creatures. I wrote:

WAITING AND READING PSALM 139:13 & 14.

For many of our friends who haven't darkened the door of a church in years
(if ever), it forced them to crack open a Bible (or more likely Google) to
search for the following words from the book of Psalms:

> *For it was you who formed my inward parts;*
> *you knit me together in my mother's womb.*
> *I praise you, for I am fearfully and wonderfully made.*
> *Wonderful are your works;*
> *that I know very well.*[11]

10. Bonhoeffer, *Letters and Papers*, 459.

11. Psalm 139:13–14, *NIV*.

As Christians, we understand human beings to be part of God's created order. The question of "Who am I?" is tied to what we call the doctrine of creation. Long before we have to figure out who we are, the Bible says that we are God's dream—fearfully and wonderfully made. As Daniel Migliorie writes,

> To speak of the world as God's creation is first of all to make an affirmation about God. By calling God the "creator" and everything that constitutes the world "creatures," Christian faith affirms the radical otherness, transcendence, and lordship of God. There is, in other words, an ontological difference between God and the world, creator and creation. . . . But to confess that God is creator is to say more. It is to say that the free, transcendent God is generous and welcoming. God was not compelled to create the world. It is an act of free grace.[12]

Discovering an answer to "Who am I?" involves a deep understanding that we are all a creation of a sovereign God, an act of free grace. Responding to this act of free grace has been summarized in the church over the years with the word *baptism*. Coming to this discovery leads us to the next question, "Who is Jesus?" or as the Apostle Paul reminds us:

> Have you forgotten that when we were baptized into union with Christ Jesus we were baptized into his death? By that baptism into his death we were buried with him, in order that, as Christ was raised from the dead by the glorious power of the Father, so also we might set out on a new life.[13]

---

12. Migliorie, *Faith Seeking Understanding*, 85.

13. Romans 6:3–4, *NIV.*

Q3—PART TWO: WHO IS JESUS?

"No one else holds...the place in the heart of the world which Jesus holds. Other gods have been as devoutly worshipped; no other man has been so devoutly loved."

—John Knox

"Why would Jesus go so far out of his way for this?" I thought to myself as our motor coach pulled up outside of the historical site known in the Bible as Caesarea Philippi. It was almost thirty miles from the Sea of Galilee with which we associate so much of Jesus' adult ministry. Why would Jesus walk all this way with his disciples in order to ask them questions he could have asked at relaxing seaside in Capernaum? The Bible records the interaction between Jesus and his disciples like this:

> Now when Jesus came into the district of Caesarea Philippi, he asked his disciples, "Who do people say that the Son of Man is?" And they said, "Some say John the Baptist, but others Elijah, and still others Jeremiah or one of the prophets." He said to them, "But who do you say that I am?" Simon Peter answered, "You are the Messiah, the Son of the living God." And Jesus answered him, "Blessed are you, Simon son of Jonah! For flesh and blood has not revealed this to you, but my Father in heaven. And I tell you, you are Peter, and on this rock I will build my church, and the gates of Hades will not prevail against it. I will give you the keys of the kingdom of heaven, and whatever you bind on earth will be bound in heaven, and whatever you loose on earth will be loosed in heaven." Then he sternly ordered the disciples not to tell anyone that he was the Messiah.[14]

Jesus leads his disciples on a long journey in order to ask them two questions, "Who do *people* say the Son of Man is?" and "Who do *you* say that I am?" Like a politician consulting the pollsters, Jesus asks his "advisors" what the public opinion is on his public image. The answer is predictable. If it was a political advisor today they'd say, "People see you as a new George Washington or Sir John A. MacDonald. You are seen to be an echo of an Abraham Lincoln or a William Lion Mackenzie King—a real visionary like

---

14. Matthew 16:13–20, *NIV.*

FDR." Jesus then makes it personal. Put the polling stats down, people. "Who do *you* say that I am?"

Walking along the pathways of Caesarea Philippi the first time I wondered, "Why would Jesus go so far out of his way for this?" And then the other shoe dropped. I realized that Caesarea Philippi in Jesus' day was the home of a pagan temple known as the Temple of Pan. Jesus led his disciples on a long hike so that Simon could make his famous confession that gave him the title "the Rock" long before any professional wrestler claimed it. Peter says, "You are the Messiah, the Son of the *living* God." I love that. Jesus led his disciples to a place littered with idols to dead small "g" gods, asks them some pop culture questions about his ministry and then things get real serious, real personal. Simon "the Rock" Peter gets the A+ answer declaring Jesus to be Messiah, or Anointed One, the Son of the Living God standing amongst dead, false gods. Brilliant. Why would Jesus go so far out of his way for this? Missional leadership in a culture of affluence knows that Jesus goes to extreme lengths for each and every one of us. Missional leadership in a culture of affluence helps turn people towards a mirror not for the sake of the latest cosmetic treatment or weight loss program but to have them understand that "Jesus goes so far out of his way *for this!*" Missional leadership in a culture of affluence brokers no deal with unbelief or with the domestication of the gospel that is so prevalent in Western culture. No, missionary disciples take seriously C. S. Lewis's classic argument in *Mere Christianity:*

> I am trying here to prevent anyone saying the really foolish thing that people often say about Him: I'm ready to accept Jesus as a great moral teacher, but I don't accept his claim to be God. That is the one thing we must not say. A man who was merely a man and said the sort of things Jesus said would not be a great moral teacher. He would either be a lunatic—on the level with the man who says he is a poached egg—or else he would be the Devil of Hell. You must make your choice. Either this man was, and is, the Son of God, or else a madman or something worse. You can shut him up for a fool, you can spit at him and kill him as a demon or you can fall at his feet and call him Lord and God, but let us not come with any patronizing nonsense about his being a great human teacher. He has not left that open to us. He did not intend to.[15]

15. Lewis, *Mere Christianity,* 51–52 (MacMillan ed.).

C. S. Lewis's teaching attempts to force human beings to decide that when Jesus aligns himself intimately with God, as the revelation at Caesarea Philippi discloses, we are forced to declare Jesus as liar, lunatic, or Lord. "Jesus is Lord" is one of the earliest recorded statements of Christian faith and in a culture of affluence we know that it is so easy to substitute "Jesus" with our mortgage, profession, reputation, bank savings, addictions, and just about anything else. The confession of Jesus is Lord, however, acknowledges that Jesus is Savior and rescuer of the whole world. The whole language of "Jesus saves" sets some people on edge. I have a hunch that for some, it conjures up imagery of a street preacher wielding a Bible like a sword as wary pedestrians give a wide berth. So how can we get a handle on this electrifying, transformative, and essential statement of faith?

As Christians we talk about the "incarnation of God" in Jesus at Christmas. If it's a midnight service we read from the prologue to John's gospel, "In the beginning was the Word, and the Word was with God and the Word was God."[16] Of course, if it is the early Christmas Eve service proclaiming the arrival of the Word of God with skin on looks a little bit different. It usually involves a little boy or girl dressed as Gabriel with crooked wings announcing to a bathrobe-clad Mary that she will bear a son called Jesus—or Yeshua—which literally means "salvation" or "God to the rescue." The kind of saving that Jesus offers is not a passive or casual saving, like tossing a few spare coins into a piggy bank. No, this is high-drama saving, more like a Coast Guard search-and-rescue helicopter hovering over a floundering ship off the coast, in the midst of a raging storm at sea. This kind of rescue is risky, urgent, and happening everywhere, all the time.

But what does Jesus save us from? For too long in the Christian tradition, the short answer was that Jesus saves us from "H-E-double hockey sticks," as those of us who grew up playing hockey on the prairies liked to call it. This fear-based approach to salvation is summed up in the bumper sticker "Jesus is taking reservations for eternity. Will it be smoking or non-smoking?"

And yet, in pastoral ministry, I have prayed that Jesus might save people from hell. Not the overheated underworld depicted so brilliantly in *Far Side* cartoons, but rather hell on earth: sitting as a pastor with someone whose marriage is crumbling under the weight of lies and infidelity; listening to a church member speak in hushed tones of sexual abuse endured in childhood; holding the hand of a dying person who is alone and regretting

16. John 1:1, *NIV.*

family estrangement that will not be undone in time; watching a wonderful person slip once again under the spell of addictions; standing at a grave beside a young widow and her children uncertain as to what the future will hold. Oh, there is certainly a need for Jesus to save us from hell on earth.

But what about those folks for whom life is just fine, ticking along comfortably without any supposed need of Jesus and his saving power? What about those who are under the spell of a culture of affluence and who have bought into the Laodicean lies of this world's material promises? What might Jesus save them from?

I was reminded of this challenge while boarding an Air Canada flight home to Vancouver from Calgary. As I found my seat, I noticed a well-known Canadian celebrity in the row behind talking loudly on his cell-phone for all to hear. As I fumbled with my seat belt, I could not help but hear this man shout at his agent, "You tell that radio show host that I'll never do another interview with him. And tell the CBC television anchorman that next time he needs to show me more respect." As I tried to engage the passenger beside me in polite conversation, it sounded like the agent at the other end of the phone was attempting, in vain, to soothe the man. Finally, the celebrity screamed into the phone, "You don't understand. *I am the center of the universe!*" The passengers around me were speechless except for the woman beside me, who rolled her eyes, leaned over, and said to me in a thick Newfoundland accent, "Boy, somebody needs to save that guy *from himself!*"

In short, Jesus saves us from ourselves and from the numerous and intoxicating small-g gods of this culture. Jesus saves us from a too-small vision of this world and our place in it. Jesus, with deep love, whispers, "You are the light of the world, you are the salt of the earth, the kingdom of God has drawn near." In a culture of affluence, missionary leaders recognize the need for the gospel story to trump card the narratives of consumerism and materialism all around. As Richard Bauckham wonders,

> What do we really need in order to recognize and to resist this new metanarrative of globalization? Surely a story that counters the global dominance of the profit-motive and the culture of consumption with a powerful affirmation of the universal values? But the Christian metanarrative can adopt this role only if it resists become a tool of the force of domination.[17]

17. Bauckham, *Bible and Mission*, 97.

In the end, it's the deep and abiding love of Christ that offers us a different and better story to live by, and in turn, saves us as disciples for the gospel mission of blessing and mending God's broken and beloved world.

Wrestling with the question of "Who is Jesus?" involves articulating our own answer to the question, "What does Jesus save us from?" and "What does Jesus save us for?" If Jesus saves us from ourselves, and this world's intoxicating but ultimately empty dreams of self-fulfillment and satisfaction, how do we mark the transition into living aligned with what Jesus saves us for? In short, the church replies, "Baptism." As Matthew records:

> Then Jesus came from Galilee to John at the Jordan, to be baptized by him. John would have prevented him, saying, "I need to be baptized by you, and do you come to me?" But Jesus answered him, "Let it be so now; for it is proper for us in this way to fulfill all righteousness." Then he consented. And when Jesus had been baptized, just as he came up from the water, suddenly the heavens were opened to him and he saw the Spirit of God descending like a dove and alighting on him. And a voice from heaven said, "This is my Son, the Beloved, with whom I am well pleased."[18]

That's what makes the question "Who is Jesus?" so fascinating. It's not engaging a concept or idea but rather encountering a person whose presence changes our lives for good and calls us beloved. Beloved. For the high school overachiever who never seems to do well enough to gain her parents attention. Beloved. For the awkward kid who is always picked on at school and always picked last for sports. Beloved. For the teen who looks in the mirror and hates the image staring back. Beloved. For the restaurant server working for minimum wage while trying her best to support her kids. Beloved. For the highly pressured salesperson who only sees their worth in monthly sales reports. Beloved. For the parent who lies awake at night worried about her teenagers and feeling like a failure in parenting. Beloved. For the empty nesters trying to figure out what purpose life may have with more years behind than ahead. Beloved. For the retiree who realizes that most friendships were connected to their employment as they watch their world get very small. Beloved. For the senior who sits all day by the phone waiting for a loved one to call. Beloved.

Discovering that the answer to "Who is Jesus?" comes with a life-altering decision we need to make can be overwhelming. Accepting the gospel truth that no matter who we are. No matter what we've done. No

18. Matthew 3:13–17, *NIV*.

matter what we fear. No matter what other people say—Jesus as the Messiah, the Son of the *Living* God, whispers beloved, beloved, beloved.

Missional leadership today takes seriously the need to help people take steps towards faith in Jesus. In a post-Christendom world, no one is "born Christian" and so disciples are made with intention and long-term commitment on behalf of the mission community or congregation. Engaging the question of "Who is Jesus?" inevitably leads people to wrestle with concepts of mission, evangelism, conversion and discipleship. Far from succumbing to the individualistic leaning of our consumerist culture, missional leaders help communities understand that whoever Jesus is—he is the same for all of us. As Karl Barth once wrote, "Jesus Christ is for me precisely—no more, no less, and no other than—what he was, is and will be, always and everywhere, for the church . . . and for the whole world."[19]

MISSION

As has been argued earlier, missional leadership understands that the church does not have a mission; rather *God's mission has a church*. It has always puzzled me that given what the sovereign God could accomplish alone, the Triune God invites us as sinful and fallible creatures to come alongside and participate in mission with that simple invitation to discipleship, "Come and follow me." The church is the instrument of God's mission in the world. As we noted in the last chapter, there is often confusion between mission and evangelism. David Bosch offers this concise definition of mission as the

> Total task that God has set the church for the salvation of the world. In its missionary involvement, the church steps out of itself, into the wider world. It crosses all kinds of frontiers and barriers: geographical, social, political, ethnic, cultural, religious, ideological. Into all these areas the church-in-mission carries the message of God's salvation. Ultimately, then, mission means being involved in the redemption of the universe and the glorification of God.[20]

Today, we are keenly aware of missional mistakes like the residential school partnership between the Canadian government and churches that led to physical and sexual abuse, imposition of Western values, and near

19. Barth, *Final Testimonies*, 13.

20. Chilcote, ed., *Study of Evangelism*, 9.

destruction of First Nations cultures. There is no way to defend the indefensible. As John Bowen so wisely states, mission should mean love but "over the centuries that basic meaning has often been encrusted with other meanings: mission as imperialism, mission as assimilation, mission as violence. Where those alien meanings came from is a matter for historians to research and for Christians to mourn."[21] Therefore, if we define mission as the church's partnership with God in the redemption of the whole world through the victory of the cross and empty grave, then we need to be clear as well about the more narrow definition of evangelism.

EVANGELISM

In an earlier chapter we turned to David Bosch for assistance in marking the difference between mission and evangelism. Bosch clarified that evangelism is that dimension and activity of the church's mission which seeks to offer every person, everywhere, a valid opportunity to be directly challenged by the gospel of explicit faith in Jesus Christ, with a view to embracing him as Savior, becoming a living member of his community, and being enlisted in his service of reconciliation, peace, and justice on earth.[22]

As discussed earlier, the best way to engage in this ministry of evangelism is through a witness in the local mission community rather than the "Lone Ranger" approach to making disciples. Evangelism is relational and it is community based. The earlier working definition of evangelism holds true. Evangelism is *a congregational process that helps people witness to their trust in Jesus, and by the Spirit's power, transforms them within community into disciples of Christ who participate in God's saving mission for the world.*

From a missional leadership perspective and as a preacher, I find it wise to pay attention to St. Augustine's argument (borrowed from Cicero) that preaching serves three purposes—to delight, instruct, and persuade. While some teachings of the church in post-Christendom may be delightful and even instructive, the sent people of God must also be persuasive. Indeed, if the church's attempt to answer "Who is Jesus?" were only delightful and instructive the church's proclamation ministry in a post-Christendom world could be called edifying but certainly not evangelistic. The key step is Augustine's third purpose—to persuade. As John's gospel concludes, "these are written so that you may come to believe that Jesus is the Messiah, the

21. Bowen, ed., *Green Shoots*, 3.
22. Bosch, *Transforming Mission*, 17.

Son of God, and that through believing you may have life in his name."[23] My colleague Stephen Farris argues that the proper desire of all preaching should be directed towards conversion, although the very language of conversion is problematic in mainline North American denominations today.[24] While the church's witness to the resurrection and its attempt to answer "Who is Jesus?" works with God's Spirit to bring about justification in a human's life before God, we first need to investigate the groundwork for that life-transforming event through the practice of invitation.

Theologically, while working towards the practice of invitation to discipleship, one must trust in the doctrine of prevenient grace.[25] While many mainline Christians today desire to create a space where it is "okay to belong before you believe," at some point seekers must be encouraged to take steps towards faith in Jesus resulting in the assurance of God's grace for their lives in light of Christ's life, death, and resurrection. How one goes about issuing that invitation is crucial. If mission communities today seek to answer for the world "Who is Jesus?" and persuade others to choose Christ over other competing idols of belief and trust in society, they must do so in ways that connect with the postmodern person. A former professor of mine, David Bartlett, described it as like "wooing a listening audience, not forcing people to 'take it or leave it.'" This wooing, or gentle persuasion, is quite different from the abrupt "turn or burn" approach still practiced in many churches today. Through my practice of ministry from coast to coast, I discovered that mission communities committed to offering an invitation to discipleship must do so regularly, in order to give individuals an opportunity to respond when they feel the nudge, or persuasion, of the Spirit. In other words, one may have to hear the invitation several times before it actually connects with their place on the faith journey. A survey in the 1990s revealed that half of the new Christians in Canada who were

---

23. John 20:31, *NIV.*

24. Farris, *Preaching that Matters*, 12.

25. An example of strong believer in prevenient grace was revivalist John Wesley (1703–1791). He believed that God's prevenient grace was present from birth and prepared us for new life in Christ. For Wesley, prevenient grace was God's divine love that surrounds all humanity and precedes any and all of our conscious impulses. Wesley wrote in his sermon "On Working Out our Own Salvation" that prevenient grace elicits, "the first wish to please God, the first dawn of light concerning His will, and the first slight transient conviction of having sinned against Him."

interviewed said they heard the gospel at least ten times or more before they made their decision for Christ.[26]

Therefore, if a missional approach to an invitation to discipleship is a slow and repetitive process, then certain assumptions about the church's evangelistic attempt to answer "Who is Jesus?" must be rethought. John Bowen offers a helpful image when it comes to our evangelistic proclamation and the practice of invitation. Bowen invites us to imagine a continuum that looks like this:

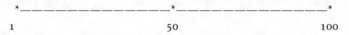

Bowen suggests that everyone in the world is on a continuum of 1 to 100 in terms of their getting to know God. No one is at 0 since, as we asserted earlier with the doctrine of prevenient grace, because of what God has done for us in Jesus no one is outside the love of God even if they don't know it. While some may like to think they have reached 100 on the graph it is only in the life to come when we see God face to face that we will be able to say regarding our journey of faith and discipleship, "it is finished." Bowen suggests that 50 is the point when a person realizes that Jesus is the key to getting to know God, and they begin to follow him. With this image now firmly in our mind Bowen argues

> Much evangelistic effort goes into trying to get people to cross that line from 49 to 50. But it is clear that there is little point in talking to someone as if they are at 49 if they are only at 17. What the person really needs is an invitation to move to 18. Of course, this makes the whole thing sound very mechanical. The way God draws us is much more relational, and our response is much more devious and messy than this image suggests. . . . Nevertheless, you get the point: coming to faith is a gradual process, and Christ-like evangelism will respect that.[27]

In light of Bowen's work we can now see that our missional leadership that includes evangelism must include a regular and varied invitation to discipleship so that we encourage people to continue to move in a Christ-ward direction whether they consider themselves Christian or not. In addition, this approach to evangelism is also a source of strength and blessing to those hurt and broken souls in our mission communities who, due to a

26. Bowen, *Evangelism for Normal People*, 83.

27. Ibid.

sudden loss or crisis of faith, have slipped back "past the 50 mark" and are floundering in their assurance of grace. This kind of invitational proclamation in light of the question "Who is Jesus?" is critical in our postmodern, postcolonial, post-Christendom, post-everything environment. As Ronald Allen argues, "Churches need to find ways that the sermon can perform one of its oldest evangelistic tasks—inviting people to the decision of whether or not to accept the love of God through Christ as the basis for their self-understanding."[28]

Missional leadership acknowledges that the Spirit of God is sending us as witnesses to the resurrection into a culture that has changed, and is changing, dramatically, and will not be kind to churches that long simply to maintain the status quo. For example, theologian Marcus Borg offers a convincing assessment of the current state of the mainline churches in North America. Borg argued,

> Until 40 years ago there was a cultural expectation that everyone would belong to a church. So long as there was this cultural expectation in place, mainline denominations did very well because they offered a culturally respectable way of being Christian. If you were mainline no one would ask you to do anything too weird, and there was a kind of community respect in the mainline denominations. Roughly 40 years ago that changed . . . so that people born after the year 1963 have grown up in a culture where that expectation has vanished. Mainline churches, as a result, have declined. Now mainline churches are a mixture of people who became Christian for conventional reasons a half century or more ago, and people who have come in later because they are intentional about the Christian life. . . . We're only about 20 years away from the time when the only people left in mainline churches will be those who are there with intentionality.[29]

Borg hints at both the historically powerful influence of culture in making disciples and the new reality that brings younger people to faith through choice, not cultural conditioning. One could easily argue a step further that in the growing secular Canadian context today, the culture is actually working *against* people making a public declaration of faith in Jesus Christ.[30] It

28. Allen, *Preaching and Practical Ministry*, 106.

29. Borg, "Being Christian in the 21st Century," http://www.homileticsonline.com/subscriber/interviews/borg.asp.

30. Statistics Canada records data on Canadian's religious identity once every ten years. The 2001 national census by Statistics Canada revealed a record high 16 percent of

is okay to say Monday morning at the office water cooler in Toronto that one went to the movies or a Leafs game Saturday night, but watch out for the stares and judgment if that same person mentions their active involvement Sunday morning at church. As Stanley Saunders and Charles Campbell suggest, "Most of us do not feel much discomfort reading the Bible in church on Sunday morning, but we may experience acute embarrassment about the prospect of reading the Bible at the mall or in the workplace."[31] As theologian Douglas John Hall notes, "The Christendom into which I was born . . . no longer exists—pockets and vestiges of it notwithstanding. Few people in the Western world today are 'caused' to be Christians by the sheer accident of birth. Many may start out that way, but fewer and fewer find inherited Christianity reason enough to stay Christian."[32]

The days are over when leaders in the mainline Christian church could rely on the mainstream culture to tell the old, old story of Jesus and his love. In many ways this is a good thing. This cultural conditioning combined with institutional inertia may have repopulated the pews generation after generation but it certainly did not strengthen our skills for inviting people to make a commitment to proclaim Jesus as Lord and apprentice as his disciple as in the days of the early church. The gospel call to "Go therefore and make disciples of all nations, baptizing them in the name of the Father and of the Son and of the Holy Spirit, and teaching them to obey everything that I have commanded you" is now back in the proper hands of the church—the sent people of God.[33] This paradigm shift in the culture around us, however, highlights the incredible need for missional leadership that recognizes both the importance of, and the unique skill set required for, evangelistic proclamation in our postmodern world. Just as the risen Christ invited his friends to join him on the lakeshore for breakfast in John 21, so too our witnessing to the resurrection invites and enables others to offer their "Yes" to God's grace-filled invitation to "Come and taste the grace eternal, come and see that God is good."[34] Without a doubt, the era of the culture making Christians is over. Whether we are comfortable or not, the epoch of inviting people to become disciples of Jesus by choice and not cultural conditioning has begun.

Canadians now claim no religious identity, up from 1 percent in 1971.

31. Saunders and Campbell, *Word on the Street,* 88.

32. Hall, *Why Christian?,* 14.

33. Matthew 28:19–20, *NRSV.*

34. Dunstan, "All who hunger," 534.

And what a curious decision it is on God's part to entrust the spread of the gospel to human beings with such a checkered past. As Stephen Farris suggests, there is profound "strangeness . . . in the notion that the God of the galaxies and the atoms speaks through weak and limited humans like us!"[35] Perhaps even stranger is that God chooses to wait on us as frail and fallible creatures to extend this most important invitation to relationship on God's behalf. When understood in this light we begin to appreciate once again the immense honor and daunting privilege that our ministry as missionary disciples truly involves. Discovering the revelation to "Who is Jesus?" and now knowing that it comes with a life altering relationship with the Triune God, we are commissioned to be Christ's witnesses to the ends of the earth.

CONVERSION

From congregational ministry to courts of presbytery and beyond, conversion, like evangelism, is seen as a dirty word, something that "those other churches talk about." And yet, if we are to fully engage in missional leadership we must reclaim and recast the word *conversion* in our theological lexicon. Part of our discomfort with the word *conversion* is likely due to the way it has been used as the crescendo in an off-key, and off-putting, evangelistic appeal that many can find Sunday mornings on cable television with a wild-eyed preacher, in a high quality suit, singing a dark song full of hellfire and brimstone. As Karl Barth bristled in response to hearing evangelist Billy Graham speak, "He acted like a madman and what he presented was certainly not the gospel . . . . It was the gospel at gunpoint . . . . It was illegitimate to make the gospel law or to 'push' it like an article for sale. . . . We must leave the good God freedom to do his own work."[36]

In response to the kind of experience Barth had of evangelism, mainline Protestant churches in particular have become uncomfortable with conversion and many leaders have tailored their ministry and preaching to avoid such unpopular or even "unseemly" experiences. Much like Marcion playing "cut and paste" with the Scriptures to suit his own inclinations, those of us in leadership roles within mainline Protestant churches should be careful that we are not simply accommodating the gospel to the culture. As my colleague at Carey College Jonathan Wilson argues,

35. Farris, *Preaching That Matters*, 7.
36. Busch, *Karl Barth*, 446.

> When the church faithfully proclaims the presence of the kingdom in the language of the world, it does not trim the gospel of the kingdom to fit the world's expectations. To preach the gospel of the kingdom so that it may be understood is not the same as preaching the gospel so that we may be liked. The church in the world faces continually the temptation to be liked by the world. But because it is not of the world, the church is continually recalled to the knowledge that we are already loved unconditionally by God in Jesus Christ.[37]

It may, in fact, come as some surprise to mainline leaders to learn that conversion is becoming an equally problematic issue in the broader Christian church as well. Robert Webber suggests that even the evangelical community is coming to terms with the unhealthy emphasis it has placed on getting converts (who may shoot up quickly but get choked by weeds or scorched by the midday sun) rather than making disciples with a lifelong commitment to Christ and his church.[38] As Bryan Stone argues, "much of contemporary evangelism, disciplined as it is by modern social imaginations with the autonomous individual at its center, is orientated toward a model in which conversion is presented as preceding incorporation into the church and the result of conviction and persuasion sufficient to convince the individual to 'decide' to convert."[39]

Indeed, missional leadership in a culture of affluence requires a strong evangelistic impulse since it offers a strong critique of the typical modern, consumerist, Western notion of an individual making decisions in a "me and my Jesus" approach to Christianity that has encouraged the prosperity gospel preaching that is so prevalent today. Stone is correct, therefore, in suggesting that evangelism is community based and looks more like an apprentice model than a Lone Ranger approach to ministry. As Stone argues, "One of the reasons that conversion is a matter of formation over time is that it is not simply a decision or an experience but the acquisition of a way of life that is embodied and passed along in community."[40]

Locating conversion back in the ebb and flow of a mission community may be the first step to reclaiming this powerful theological concept for the missional church in North America. We hear an echo of Martin Luther's

37. Wilson, *God So Loved*, 176.
38. Webber, *Ancient Future Evangelism*, 13.
39. Stone, *Evangelism after Christendom*, 263.
40. Ibid., 259.

belief that "the one who wants to find Christ must first find the church."[41] Missional leadership that makes evangelism and its hoped-for outcome of conversion a priority rooted within a Christian community but roots that practice within community will be challenging to many established viewpoints of evangelism. As Brad Kallenberg writes:

> My suggestion that the intelligibility of the gospel depends strongly upon the character of the believing community may be disconcerting to Christians who, perhaps because they are steeped in individualism, cannot help but construe evangelism as a matter of one-on-one conversations. I am not advocating that we cease to have face-to-face conversations with individuals about the claim Jesus makes on our lives. Rather, I am suggesting that such conversations will not make complete sense to unbelievers who don't have a clue what difference Jesus makes for the way Christians live with one another.[42]

If Stephen Farris is correct that the desire of the church's witness should be focused on people's conversion and salvation, then how in our evangelism should a missional leader work towards that goal? We have already established that as the sent people of God, evangelism is in response to, and by the power, of the Holy Spirit alone. Whatever we may "do" in our evangelism for conversion it is only in light of what the Holy Spirit is already "doing" in the life of individual and the community. Commenting on the role of the sermon in adult conversion, Frank Honeycutt encourages preachers to remember the great revivalist Jonathan Edwards' advice in his 1740 sermon, "The Reality of Conversion," where after listing sixteen specific things someone might do to effect adult conversion Edwards adds a final comment, "Take heed that you don't trust either in anything that you have done or can do for, when you have done all, you have done nothing, nothing that can make any atonement for the least of your sins or that is worthy to be offered as a price for the least of God's favors."[43]

With this clarity regarding the role of the Holy Spirit we acknowledge that the mission community must be formed to be hospitable to newcomers, creating a space that enables people to belong before they believe. Next, a missional community seeks to illuminate and educate the hearts and

---

41. Ibid., 263. Here we could also turn to John Calvin who, drawing on Augustine and Ambrose, said that we could not know God as Father were it not for Mother Church.

42. Kallenberg, *Live to Tell*, 50.

43. Honeycutt, *Preaching for Adult Conversion*, 158.

minds of newcomers to the gospel truth and its claims about "Who is Jesus?" We also know that we must witness to the resurrection with invitation to discipleship often, so that the call may be heard many times throughout one's spiritual development. And yet, there is no neat system or method for the harvest. Instead, Scripture simply encourages us to call on the Lord of the harvest and wait for the results. Indeed, conversion may be a sudden thing like Paul on the road to Damascus for some in our churches; however, my experience has been that people need to be nurtured in the faith over a long period of time before they become disciples of Christ. While some may experience Paul's "deep fryer faith" it is more likely that our evangelistic preaching ministry will result in conversions that resemble the "slower cooker faith" of someone like John Wesley who spent his whole life in the church and was ordained over a decade before he felt his "heart strangely warmed."[44] In North American churches, however, I have often found an attitude amongst church leaders that expects too little from potential converts and accepts a conversion process that in the end results in only "half-baked Christians." Latin American scholar Orlando Costas reminds us that conversion, biblically speaking, involves both, "repentance, or a change of mind, and faith toward God."[45] Regarding repentance, Costas warns:

> Instead of confronting men and women with their sin as manifested in their concrete social situations, the church has much too often confronted them with their abstract sinfulness, leaving their sinful relations to their particular life situations unaffected. Instead of confronting people with the demands of Christ, the church has accommodated the gospel to their own way of thinking and living.[46]

Conversion, however, from Athens to Aldersgate to the Americas today, is surely more than simply an intellectual assent to the claims of Christ whether that be a dramatic or slow process. As Bryan Stone argues,

> Conversion is much more than an individual's deciding to believe new pieces of information that she or he now possesses. It occurs at the level of one's convictions, which . . . are so central to one's character as a person that a change in them would involved a change (would, indeed be a change) in that person's character. . . .

44. Lockhart, *Gen X, Y Faith?*, 52.

45. Costas, "Evangelism and the Gospel of Salvation" in Chilcote, ed., *The Study of Evangelism*, 42.

46. Ibid., 43.

> In conversion, the whole person is remade—heart, mind, body, relationships, allegiances, habits. In essence, a new identity is acquired . . . .[47]

Therefore, missional leaders clarify the gospel, join newcomers in the community and include them in Christian fellowship, and by announcing the kingdom of God's arrival in Jesus Christ anticipate real change in the listener's lives. As Dietrich Bonhoeffer once said, "When Christ calls a man, he bids him come and die."[48] When missional theology engages the world evangelistically we recognize that through the Holy Spirit's power there can be a real change in the listener, a dying and rising in not just their intellectual understanding of faith but the ethical standards by which they live in the world. Anna Carter Florence is quick to remind us, however, that the change is not limited to the listener and can transform the leader as well.

Specifically commenting on preaching, Florence argues, "The goal of preaching is not consensus . . . . The goal of preaching is conversion—the preacher's conversion. The preacher models conversion by engaging the text at a deeper level in order to be formed by it (or by the Other, which is God)."[49] Brad Kallenberg suggests that conversion involves the old Hebrew understanding of repentance as turning (*shuv*) rather than the more widely known Greek understanding of a light-switch repentance as a change of mind (*metanoia*).[50] According to Kallenberg, this turning or conversion that moves people from a pre-existing lifestyle to a new one influenced by the gospel and Christian community results in a change of one's social identity, the acquisition of a new conceptual language, and the shifting of one's paradigm.[51]

Coming to terms with this new postmodern understanding of conversion is easier in light of the emerging church movement moving across North America and Europe. As Brian McLaren, one of the emerging church leaders, commented on conversion at his church:

> We don't do "sinner's prayers" . . . or make a big deal about "When did you 'get saved?'" The whole language of punctiliar salvation is problematic for ministry in a postmodern context, I think. Instead, we talk about becoming followers of Christ. We're very

47. Stone, *Evangelism after Christendom*, 262.

48. Bonhoeffer, *Cost of Discipleship*, 89.

49. Florence, *Preaching as Testimony*, 108.

50. Kallenberg, *Live to Tell*, 70.

51. Ibid., 32.

reticent about using evangelical jargon, not just because we think it's easily misunderstood, but also because we think it is often sub-biblical in its modernism. . . . The gospel is too often a story about how people can go to heaven rather than hell when they die. But I think we've got to realize that that isn't what the gospel is really about. The gospel isn't about how Jesus saves individual souls from hell. The gospel is about how Jesus saves the world.[52]

Dan Kimball echoes McLaren, writing, "Emerging generations are connecting with the idea of living in tune with Jesus, placing yourself under God's reign and being a participant in the kingdom now."[53] Kimball warns that with emerging generations conversion may be a lot messier and take a lot longer than in previous generations since, "In past generations, when a non-Christian converted, they generally already had a biblical world-view. . . . But with emerging generations, many times we are dealing with a total change of their concept of God, morals . . . and so on."[54]

Rob Bell cautions that Christian conversion attempts often lack the grace-filled love of the Christ from whom the invitation is properly extended. Bell warns in his book *Velvet Elvis,*

Oftentimes the Christian community has sent the message that we love people and build relationships in order to convert them to the Christian faith. So there is an agenda. And when there is an agenda, it isn't really love, is it? It's something else. We have to rediscover love, period. Love that loves because it is what Jesus teaches us to do. We have to surrender our agendas. Because some people aren't going to become Christians like us no matter how hard we push. They just aren't. And at some point we have to commit them to God, trusting that God loves them more than we ever could. I obviously love to talk to people about Jesus and my faith. I'll take every opportunity I can get. But I have learned that when I toss out my agenda and simply love as Jesus teaches me to, I often end up learning more about God than I could have imagined.[55]

Perhaps here we find a new understanding of conversion that is rooted in the love and joy of the mission community. That deep sense of community comes from our understanding that answering "Who is Jesus?" leads us, by grace and God's adoption, into the ultimate community of Father, Son, and

52. McLaren, as quoted in Kallenberg, ibid., 69–71.
53. Kimball, *Emerging Church*, 282.
54. Ibid., 288.
55. Bell, *Velvet Elvis*, 167.

Holy Spirit. It is our confession and conviction of the Triune God's community essence that helps us pattern our own lives and communities in light of the agape, self-giving love of Father, Son, and Holy Spirit. As Craig Van Gelder reminds us, "A missional imagination needs to be deeply informed by Trinitarian foundations, from both the Western tradition, which focuses on the *sending* character of God, and the Eastern tradition, which focuses more on the *social reality* within the Godhead."[56] Conversion no longer becomes something that we *do* to others, but rather it is something we delight in experiencing *through* others as we meet them in the community as the sent people of God, as they join in our fellowship, hear the teachings of Jesus, and respond in their own time to the invitation to discipleship. Peter Rollins picks up on this shift when he writes that Christianity involves a process of journey and becoming where being a Christian always involves becoming a Christian, since

> We need not look far to find that our religious communities influenced as they are by the movement known as modernity, have tended to emphasize the idea of "being" and "destination": one becomes a Christian, joins a church and is saved. From this idea of destination flows our understanding of evangelism as a means of sharing our faith and encouraging others to embrace it for themselves. For those involved in the emerging conversation, this view distorts the deeper meaning of evangelism, for once we acknowledge that we are becoming Christian, becoming Church and being saved, then the other can be seen as a possible instrument of our further conversion. Even a brief reflection upon the darkness in our own lives bears testimony to the fact that we need to be evangelized as much, if not more, than those around us.[57]

Tom Long summarizes this new and open understanding of conversion that applies to all members of the community whether it is the preacher or a newcomer when he writes,

> The more confident, joyful, and trusting our faith is, the less we will need others to validate our every jot and tittle. The more we will know that our testimony is ultimately about God's goodness and not about our anxious need, it is ultimately given as a gift to others and not as a self-serving attempt to put sandbags in the leaking levee of our own faith.[58]

56. Van Gelder and Zscheile, eds., *Missional Church*, 132.

57. Rollins, *Speak of God*, 5–6.

58. Long, *Testimony*, 118.

DISCIPLESHIP

Recently, I visited Israel for the third time in my life. I got up early one morning to walk along the majestic shores of the Sea of Galilee in Israel. As I dipped my feet in the cool water I tried to imagine what it must have been like the day that those hard working fishers and "synagogue school dropouts" were called by the one we call Yeshua. Simon and Andrew, as the first disciples, heard the call from the One who said, "Follow me, and I will make you fish for people."[59] As Christians we follow, and are obedient to, our Lord who calls us, claims us, and commissions us to participate in and proclaim the kingdom of God ushered in through Jesus' life, death, and resurrection. Walter Brueggemann is clear that discipleship is "not just a nice notion of church membership or church education; it entails a resituating of our lives. The disciples of Jesus are the ones who follow their master, able to do so because they have been instructed in his way of life, both his aim and practice of embodying that aim."[60] The glimpse given to us of the life of discipleship in the early church in Acts 2:42 helps to flesh out a working definition of discipleship as follows: *Discipleship is the response to Christ's gracious invitation to follow him and conform one's life to the in-breaking reign of God by devoting oneself to teaching, fellowship, breaking of bread, and prayers.* This response to God's grace-filled invitation is the outcome of God's mission, evangelism, and conversion. It is what we will explore next in answer the question, "Who am I *in* Jesus?"

Before we move onto that question, however, we pause to acknowledge the importance that the church's witness, as the sent people of God in the world, answers the question "Who is Jesus?" not simply with information but with demand. The Word of God demands a response from humanity and promises a life-altering, joyful relationship with God in Christ through the wonder of the Holy Spirit. As missional leaders in a culture of affluence, it is clear that by attempting to answer "Who is Jesus?" we are always engaged in an approximate answer. Respecting the sovereignty of God and being careful not to fall into the trap of domesticating the gospel, missional leaders recognize that it is ultimately Christ himself, crucified and risen, who defines ultimately the answer to the question, "Who is Jesus?"

59. Matthew 4:19, *NRSV.*
60. Chilcote, ed., *Study of Evangelism,* 230.

Perhaps it is best to summarize this by turning to C. S. Lewis's classic line in the Narnia series where Susan quizzes Mr. Beaver about the nature of Aslan the Lion—the Christ archetype:

> *"Aslan is a lion—the Lion, the great Lion." "Ooh" said Susan. "I'd thought he was a man. Is he—quite safe? I shall feel rather nervous about meeting a lion."*
>
> *"Safe?" said Mr Beaver . . . "Who said anything about safe? 'Course he isn't safe. But he's good. He's the King, I tell you."*[61]

WHO AM I (IN) JESUS?

Jesus's resurrection is the beginning of God's new project not to snatch people away from earth to heaven but to colonize earth with the life of heaven.

—N. T. Wright, *Surprised by Hope*

Living as a missionary disciple in this world entails acknowledging the hard work necessary in wrestling with the question, "Who am I?" This "soul" work involves deconstructing an identity the world has assigned us and leaning into the power of prevenient grace, seeing ourselves in light of the doctrine of creation—grasping through the illumination of the Holy Spirit both who and whose we are. This grasping, this searching—in God's own time—leads to a confrontation with the Word. The question "Who is Jesus?" must be addressed and we must allow the question to address us in order to enter fully into the incarnate Word revealed in empty cradle, empty cross, and empty tomb. The church's mission includes the need to translate for each generation the truth of who Jesus is for the cosmos and our own lives. Once we are washed in the waters of baptism and marked by the Holy Spirit, as Christ's own forever, there remains the question of "Who am I *in Jesus?*"

How are our lives different in light of this encounter with the incarnate Word Jesus Christ? How do our lives reflect God's holiness as we move deeper into relationship with the Father, Son, and Holy Spirit? In a "country club Christianity" held captive by Laodicean affluence, the desire

61. Lewis, *Essential C. S. Lewis*, 93.

to have our lives reflect the transformation that new life in Christ brings, seems not only unnecessary but even unseemly. But missional leadership that leans into a culture of affluence understands that the answer to the question, "Who am I *in* Jesus?" is a lifelong pursuit based not on having our needs met but in joining God in the neighborhood and participating in kingdom life *now*. It is a desire to reflect the beauty and holiness of being in Christ while gathered by God in Christian community, built up through Word and sacrament and, most importantly, sent out to be witnesses to the gospel in the places where we live, work, and play. The sending of God's people into the world is for the purpose of joining God in the ministry of reconciliation that the gospel brings—nothing less than the mending of God's broken yet beloved world. Martin Luther had a clear sense of both the joy and duty of obedience to Christ that comes through disciples involved in living out an answer to the question, "Who am I *in* Jesus?" Luther summarized the Christian life as follows, "A Christian is a perfectly free lord of all, subject to none. A Christian is a perfectly dutiful servant of all, subject of all, subject to all."[62]

The old confessions of faith speak clearly to this desire to be in Christ and in the world. The Westminster Shorter Catechism addresses the question of what is humanity's chief end or purpose by responding that we exist to "glorify God and enjoy Him forever." Surely someone living "in Christ" in this world, and clinging to that promise should stand out from the crowd? Or how about the Heidelberg Catechism's beautiful answer to its opening question, "What is your only comfort in life and death?" Our Reformed ancestors replied, "That I am not my own, but belong with body and soul, both in life and death, to my faithful Savior Jesus Christ."

In the next chapter we will explore more fully what it looks like for individuals and mission communities to "practice what they preach" as they live out what it means to know and trust "Who am I in Jesus?" For now, it is sufficient to say that being "in Christ" is not simply reading an owner's manual to a new life and hoping to put into practice a few "tips and tricks" on a better life. No, it is going deeper into a relationship in a way that a couple may explore a deeper level of trust after years of marriage or an adult child might learn to appreciate an aging parent in a whole new light. Missional leadership trusts deeply that the One who began this relationship is always out front of us in the world, inviting us to partner in practical ways that reflect love of God and neighbor. For those who follow Jesus, knowing

---

62. Luther, *On Christian Liberty*, with reference to Philippians 2.

who we are *in* Jesus means "praying attention" to what God is doing and living with an expectation of revelation. One of the most delightful Bible stories that reflect this missionary discipleship reality is a post-resurrection story in Luke's gospel.

I've always been fascinated by the stories that follow on the heels of the gospel's witness to the resurrection. In fact, in the Gospel according to Luke, the author barely takes a breath between telling us, through the lens of female followers of Christ, that the tomb was empty and placing the reader's feet firmly on the road to Emmaus. The women were at the tomb, of course, because the burial of Jesus had been rushed. He was laid to rest as the last flickers of sunlight disappeared, beginning the Jewish Sabbath where no work could be done, not even anointing a body. With the Sabbath over and the markets open, the women returned with spices early in the morning to the tomb, where Jesus' body would be left over several months to decompose before the bones would be collected and put in an ossuary. The resurrection event causes shock and confusion within the community of disciples, however. With no body present the women are speechless, Peter is speechless, but Cleopas, a follower of Jesus, is on the move. Luke records the event like this:

> Now that same day two of them were going to a village called Emmaus, about seven miles from Jerusalem. They were talking with each other about everything that had happened. As they talked and discussed these things with each other, Jesus himself came up and walked along with them; but they were kept from recognizing him.[63]

Without even pausing for a breath, Luke the storyteller has us on the road to Emmaus, an ordinary road, walking with Cleopas and another disciple. What's the other disciple's name? Well, trick question. The disciple is never named. Some feel the disciple is unnamed on purpose—so that we can feel free to substitute *our name* instead. *We* are on the road to Emmaus—a forgettable little village seven miles northwest of Jerusalem. Today, of course, there are competing claims to the "authentic Emmaus" and it's funny, but the guy working in the gift shop at each location will swear it's the *real* Emmaus. No bother: after all, the Emmaus road was just an ordinary trail leading away from Jerusalem.

As Cleopas and the other disciple walk along, they are in a heated conversation—the Greek words used here mean chitchat and discussion or

63. Luke 24:13–16, *NIV*.

debate. What are they talking about? Well, not the latest episode of *The Real Housewives of Jerusalem* that premiered during Holy Week—as interesting as that might be. No, they are talking about all that has happened in the city that week.

And then they encounter a stranger. Now, they are walking during the day because it is safer. Bandits can be found on the road if you recall the parable of the Good Samaritan, and this safe-looking stranger makes them strong—three people on the journey—on that ordinary road going to Emmaus. Now the Bible lets us in on a little secret right away—*the stranger is Jesus*—and somehow they are kept from recognizing him. Now, some people have trouble getting past this part of the story. How could they not recognize him? You should recognize your faith leader, your pastor, when you see him. I recall several years ago being at a Vancouver Canucks hockey game with my young son Jack, when I was asked by a Canucks representative if I wanted to participate in a inner tube rolling contest for prizes during the intermission on the ice. Well, of course, who doesn't want to do that? As I gingerly walked out onto the Roger's arena ice surface and rolled the silly inner tube along I could feel the texts going off on my iPhone. Later I would discovered the messages were from church members at the game saying, "I see you!" and "Why is our pastor on the ice?" and a few other delightful remarks! Whether in a pulpit or an area jumbo screen—people can recognize their faith leader. So, how could these disciples not recognize Jesus?

Well, a few years ago I was waiting in the basement of Union Station, Toronto where all the regional trains converge in the downtown of Canada's largest city. I was queued up in a long line and started chatting to a rather distinguished older-looking gentleman beside me. We talked about the weather, the NHL playoffs, and I was offering some tips on how the Toronto Maple Leafs hockey team could have done better that year. We shuffled our bags along the dirty tiled floor as the train started to board. Finally, just before we were about to board the train I stopped and said to my conversation partner, "It's been lovely chatting with you. I feel like I just have to say—you look a lot like Gordie Howe." For those of you who are not hockey fans, Gordie Howe (a.k.a. Mr. Hockey) was one of the finest players ever in the NHL. At that point, my conversation partner dropped his bag, put his hands on his hips, and said, "I AM GORDIE HOWE." I felt so, so silly. I was fortunate not to receive a famous Gordie Howe elbow to the head in the basement of the train station that day.

This lack of recognition for Jesus in the Emmaus Road story also reminds me of when I had the privilege of serving Christ in Halifax on the east coast of Canada. Naturally, the church had a large number of Navy officers in the congregation. As part of their duties, of course, Navy personnel are separated from their families for long periods of time. Like most Navy men, one officer in my church wore a beard as was permitted by regulations. He was away for six months and was called home a week early from his ship to Halifax, to attend to some naval intelligence business on shore. On a whim, he decided to shave his beard before returning home. He went home to surprise his wife but she was out and a neighbor said she was at the grocery store. As he strolled into the local grocery store they met coming around the corner and—she had absolutely no idea who he was and passed him right on by. She didn't recognize him. She wasn't expecting him. He looked different than she remembered him. Maybe it was a little like that for the disciples on the road to Emmaus. They didn't recognize Jesus because they weren't expecting him and he looked different than they remembered. Resurrection can do that to a person.

Jesus, the stranger, asks them what they are talking about and Cleopas is astounded that this guy must be the only person leaving Jerusalem who has not heard about Jesus. Cleopas pours out his heart to this stranger, sharing his deep, deep disappointment with how things turned out, essentially his disappointment with God. After all, this was not the way things were supposed to turn out.

I think Cleopas speaks for all of us when it comes to disappointment. As a pastor I have had the privilege of sitting with people in their highest moments of achievement and their darkest times of struggle. The disappointment that Cleopas speaks of, feeling betrayed by Jesus' promises, of the betrayal of his fellow disciples, and ultimately the seeming defeat of Good Friday is also a confession of disappointment in God. Cleopas is not alone in this disappointment. He's just honest enough to speak for the rest of us.

Its funny, but I find it interesting that people are often more honest about their disappointments and failures in coffee shops with friends than with brothers and sisters in Christ in church. Each week I go to a local coffee shop, sit and read the news on my iPad and enjoy a skinny latte, and eavesdrop on the conversations all around me. Eavesdropping is a missional, spiritual discipline to open up to what God is doing in other people's lives beyond the usual "churchy" conversations I usually find myself in. When listening carefully to the human narrative floating around the coffee shop I hear everything from disappointment ranging from the trivial—couldn't find a good parking spot—to the profound: disappointment in self, in the confession of how short-tempered we are with children, disappointment in the meanspirited behavior of so-called friends, disappointment in the ever so gentle distancing of relationship between husband and wife. Disappointment not only in self or others but in God as well—in the cancer diagnosis of a dear friend, of prayers unanswered, in the injustice that is obvious in this world of abundance. Listening with a theological ear you hear on people's lips doctrines like theodicy, soteriology, eschatology, and more. Of course, the answers to these doctrinal questions often come with a folk theology that leaves much to be desired. Nevertheless, it seems that ordinary, everyday North Americans are like Cleopas—also able to express disappointment in us, in others, and in God.

And then, I love what happens next. Cleopas even tells this stranger that that very day the company of women visited the tomb and found it empty, but he was disappointed since they did not see Jesus. *He says this while talking unknowingly to Jesus.* The "stranger" responds to Cleopas by pointing out how much he's missed the mark and attempts to open their minds to what God is doing in the neighborhood through a little pilgrimage Bible study on the Emmaus Road.

As they near Emmaus, Jesus appears to turn away and continue on the road. The disciples must beg him to come in for the hour was late, the road would be dangerous. It seems a bit odd that Jesus would appear to peel off at this point and head on his way. It only makes sense if you stop and think about the last time you were out for dinner with friends. What happened when the bill arrived? Did you "fight" over it with the conversation going back and forth like this, "Here, let me get the bill," to which your dining companions also offered to pay? In our contemporary social customs, it only seems right if there is a little exchange—a "tug-of-war" takes place over who will pay the bill. Finally one person gives up and the other pays the bill, right? Well, the social custom of Jesus' day was that you had to appear to be turning down the offer of hospitality. As a stranger you might say, "No thank you, I'll be just fine." To which the host insists, "No, you must come and stay with us tonight." "Well, all right," replies the stranger.

And so, Jesus enters the home in Emmaus but as soon as he is through the door, the social custom wears off. Jesus oddly takes the place at the table as host, and sits down in order to break and bless the bread. As a reader we almost instinctively feel our lips move as if we are celebrating the Lord's Supper, repeating the Eucharist language, "This is my body, given for you." It's only then, in the breaking of bread, of this first post-resurrection communion service—do this in remembrance of me—that Jesus is recognized.

The disciples' disappointment transforms into discovery as they come to terms with the astonishing truth and power of the resurrection. Their heartache turns to heartburn. They say to one another, "Weren't our hearts on fire when Jesus was walking along with us and we didn't even know it?" They rush back to Jerusalem, throwing caution to the wind with no fear of travelling at night. The power and light of the resurrected Lord is enough to lead them, almost as the Lord once went before the people of Israel in a pillar of cloud by day and a pillar of fire by night.

And they run on an ordinary road with an extraordinary story, once marked by death and sorrow, now full of life and love and laughter. They have discovered not only answers to "Who am I?' and "Who is Jesus?" but in light of the resurrection they become witnesses to God's saving power that answers definitively the question, "Who am I in Jesus?"

Seeing that we share that same post-resurrection world as the early disciples, if Jesus could appear on the Emmaus Road then why not on the ordinary road that lies outside our mission communities, workplaces, coffee shops, pubs, schools, or homes? If Jesus responded to Cleopas's disappointment without the disciple even knowing the resurrected Christ was present, what would it look like to confess our own disappointment in self, others, and God—trusting that we are heard and loved, while also living with an "expectation of revelation" all around us in the neighborhood?

If Jesus can be seen in the breaking of the bread, then we too should expect to see and feel, taste and touch something of the divine whenever we break bread in Jesus' name around a communion table, restaurant patio, or dining room furniture with friends at a dinner party. The Lord's Supper becomes God's communion with us—a catalyst, a reorientation, an eye-opening aha moment not to the world as we have seen it but to creation as God is making it. Our lives are saturated with the agape or self-giving love that we witness in the life, death, and resurrection of Jesus. Our lives reflect his glory with this self-giving love for the sake of the world he died to save.

When we seek to answer the question, "Who am I in Jesus?" we acknowledge the agape or self-giving love of God who calls us to be disciples of the risen Christ, sent forth in mission to witness to his victory over sin and death and reconciling work in the world. Who am I in Jesus? A redeemed sinner, a dedicated disciple, and an avowed apostle of Christ's movement that is moving towards consummation at the end of time. Discovering that God in Christ has made us "in Christ" to be his disciples and witnesses, should give us pause to ask what exactly this discipleship is all about. We do not do this witness as "Lone Rangers" but rather are formed for this work together with others in our local mission communities. As Dan Kimball suggests,

> Every disciple is an evangelist to some degree. Being a pastor means leading a community of not just disciples but mission-minded disciples. Evangelism needs to bleed from your entire church's being and should motivate Christians to be more hardcore disciples. A truly evangelistic church is a church that knows its Bible all the more, prays all the more, and loves people all the more. We need to be training people to share with others who Jesus is.[64]

According to Matthew's gospel Jesus called his first disciples as he strolled down the beach, reaching out to Simon and Andrew saying, "Follow me, and I will make you fish for people."[65] As Christians we follow, and are obedient to, our Lord who calls us, claims us, and commissions us to participate in, and proclaim, the reign of God ushered in through Jesus' life, death, and resurrection. Walter Brueggemann is clear that discipleship is "not just a nice notion of church membership or church education; it entails a resituating of our lives. The disciples of Jesus are the ones who follow their master, able to do so because they have been instructed in his way of life, both his aim and practice of embodying that aim."[66] Again, discipleship, the experience of being "in Christ," can be defined as *the response to Christ's gracious invitation to follow him and conform one's life to the in-breaking reign of God by devoting oneself to teaching, fellowship, breaking of bread, and prayers.*

Our post-Emmaus Road witness as disciples of the Risen Christ is a bold counterattack in this culture of affluence and apathy. As Darrell Guder argues

> The gospel is the person and work of Jesus as the salvation event towards which God's mission has been moving and from which that mission now moves into the entire world on the way to its eschatological consummation when God fulfills all his promises.

64. Kimball, *Emerging Church,* 289.
65. Matthew 4:19, *NRSV.*
66. Chilcote, ed., *Study of Evangelism,* 230.

After Easter, the apostles modified the dominical instruction given in Luke 10 when the seventy were sent out. They were instructed to announce, "The Kingdom of God has come near to you." (Luke 10:9) "The content of their proclamation is no longer only the kingdom of God which has come near, but rather the proclamation of Jesus as the Messiah and returning Lord." This risen Lord now sends his disciples into the world to carry out the Missio Dei (mission of God) that was the purpose and content of his life, death and resurrection. The mission of the Christian church is defined by the entire event of the life, teaching, proclamation, and passion of Jesus.[67]

As disciples, we are sent out onto ordinary roads with an extraordinary story to tell—the gospel is true. God is good. Christ is risen. The only question is will we accept the Holy Spirit's prompting to be brave and bold like Cleopas, pushing back from the table to run and tell others the story that God's love is greater than human hate, that life is stronger than death, that grace and forgiveness will always overcome evil in this world and the next? Who might we share this story with? Whose life is waiting to be changed? Who is ready to see what is possible when an Easter epiphany takes place and we discover who we are in Jesus Christ? As God's witnesses to the resurrection when we boldly proclaim the gospel through our mission communities in a culture of affluence, we have eyes to see, ears to hear, and hearts to love the world so that:

God is glorified
    Jesus is recognized
        The gospel is magnified
            The devil is terrified
                The church is energized
                    And all creation is sanctified.

---

67. Guder, *Continuing Conversion*, 46. Guder is referencing the words of Peter Stuhlmacher in this quote.

Chapter Eight

Five Mark' "S" of the New "Missional Community"

(Jesus) told them, "The harvest is plentiful, but the workers are few. Ask the Lord
of the harvest, therefore, to send out workers into his harvest field. Go!
I am sending you out like lambs among wolves. Do not take a purse or bag or
sandals; and do not greet anyone on the road.

—Luke 10:2–4

One of the things you learn quickly when you own a cottage on an
island is that you never call an expert to fix something you might
be able to fix yourself. Getting an experienced tradesperson to come for
repairs on an island means that the moment he or she steps off the boat
and onto your dock, you are already a couple of hundred dollars poorer.
Owning a cottage on an island turns ordinary people into MacGyver-like
characters, willing to rig up solutions to any problem with duct tape and
chicken wire. During my teenage years I spent a lot of time on the family
island playing "Mr. Fix-it" with my Uncle Jack. It was at that cottage that I
learned everything from basic plumbing and electrical work, to how to raise

up a building and the importance of a well-placed telephone post. What I discovered summer after summer, much to my naïve teenage mind, was that my Uncle Jack actually *didn't need me* at that cottage. Sure, it helped to have an extra set of hands around on a work project. What I figured out, however, after clunking around the cottage for a couple of summers, was that my Uncle Jack wanted to *teach me* the things that *he* had learned. Always the educator, my retired principal uncle saw an opportunity to pass on his wisdom, while watching me grow with skills and practices needed for a full and abundant life. It was a joy to learn as my uncle's apprentice all those summers at the cottage.

In a similar way, following the risen Christ and discovering an answer to "Who am I *in* Jesus?" means enrolling in the *school of Jesus* we call the church. In the Reformed tradition, we place a high value on the *sovereignty of God*. To say it directly, God is in charge. No committee meetings, no public opinion polls, no worries about re-election. God acts. From creation through fall to redemption (covenant to Christ) we acknowledge God at work in the world, bringing this cosmological experiment to a proper and joyful consummation in God's own time. The soteriological puzzle is that while God could clearly accomplish all by God's own sovereign power, God chooses to partner with fragile, fallible human creatures. Strange. Sounds like a risky plan to me. Like an uncle making repairs at the family cottage, God could get the job done quickly without any help but God chooses to engage another partner in order to impart knowledge and wisdom through the experience of co-creating. Again, a risky plan unless, of course, God simply delights in this relationship with humankind. A risky plan unless, of course, God as covenant maker and covenant keeper continues to reach out to humanity through sheer grace. A risky plan unless, of course, God is motivated by the desire to include humanity within the revelation of God's own experience of mutual, self-giving love found in Father, Son, and Holy Spirit.

Like an uncle reaching out to a nephew struggling to make sense of the world after his parent's untimely death, God reaches out to humanity and desires to have us pattern our lives on God's unforced rhythms of grace. Meeting us in our brokenness, accepting us just as we are but having no intention of leaving us the way God found us. Discovering who and whose we are as human creatures means that before we know it, we are enrolled in the school of Jesus we call the church with a simple invitation that may sound something like this:

> Are you tired? Worn out? Burned out on religion? Come to me.
> Get away with me and you'll recover your life. I'll show you how
> to take a real rest. Walk with me and work with me—watch how
> I do it. Learn the unforced rhythms of grace. I won't lay anything
> heavy or ill-fitting on you. Keep company with me and you'll learn
> to live freely and lightly.[1]

Missional leadership in a culture of affluence takes seriously the need for us
to claim our identity as disciples (not consumers—especially of religion!).
Our core identity as disciples or students enrolled in the school of Jesus
we call the church, means that every aspect of our lives is governed by our
relationship with the headmaster Christ. This is not simply about belief. It is
much deeper than that. Anyone can say they believe in God. Big deal. Even
the devil *believes* in God. The real question is do we *trust* in God? Do we
turn our whole lives over, daily, to God in joyful obedience to God's will? It
sounds a little bit like, "Your will be done on earth as it is in heaven." Enrollment in the school of Jesus requires not only belief in God but trust also in
God to direct and provide for us as we practice our resurrection faith. The
Apostle Paul captured it nicely when he said,

> So here's what I want you to do, God helping you: Take your ev-
> eryday, ordinary life—your sleeping, eating, going-to-work, and
> walking-around life—and place it before God as an offering. Em-
> bracing what God does for you is the best thing you can do for
> him. Don't become so well-adjusted to your culture that you fit
> into it without even thinking. Instead, fix your attention on God.
> You'll be changed from the inside out. Readily recognize what
> he wants from you, and quickly respond to it. Unlike the culture
> around you, always dragging you down to its level of immaturity,
> God brings the best out of you, develops well-formed maturity in
> you.[2]

Missional leadership in a culture of affluence takes Paul's caution seriously
to not become so well adjusted to the dominant culture that we, as Christians, fit into it without thinking. One of the ways to help equip disciples, in
the school of Jesus we call the church, to resist this dominant culture is to
teach, model, and experiment with Christian practices. Essentially, it is an
invitation to practice what we preach. The ancient church had five marks or
practices for those gathered in the school of Jesus we call the church. What

1. Matthew 11:28–30, *The Message.*
2. Romans 12:1–2, *The Message.*

follows is an attempt to revisit these five marks through contemporary practices of those who find themselves clunking around the family cottage *ecclesia* we know as the household of faith.[3]

SABBATH

As a missional leader in a culture of North American affluence, I have tried to help people moving from a pre-Christian to a Christian state of identity explore the "so what" of "Who am I in Jesus?" Much of our evangelical work involves helping people take steps towards faith in Jesus. But what happens next? The ancient marks of the church outline the basic rhythm of the Christian life we call discipleship. I have taken the liberty of renaming "Liturgia" *Sabbath* knowing full well that purists will not be pleased. No, the Christian practice of Sabbath is not the same as liturgy or "the work of the people" experienced in worship. But ever since the fourth century, when Shabbat and the Lord's Day were combined, most Christians have experienced their main liturgical gathering on the Sunday Sabbath.[4] By placing liturgica within the Sunday Sabbath, missional leaders can also expand the understanding of worship from a consumerist model of religion (i.e., a place I go to have *my* spiritual needs met) to a holistic communal practice of slowing down and acknowledging our place within creation as well as our relationship with the Creator.

Partnering with the Holy Spirit, disciples in a missional context endeavor to become more Christlike daily by joining what God is doing out ahead of them in the community through a commitment to the practice of Sabbath. A working definition of a missionary disciples commitment to Sabbath includes *a commitment to regular worship with the church family; a desire to engage practices that recreate and restore body, mind, and spirit; and a curiosity to explore the power of prayer.*

As noted above, commitment to regular worship is a critical part of keeping Sabbath. As Tom Long reminds us, "worship is a dress rehearsal for speaking faithfully in the rest of life" and so God gathers the universal body

---

3. The five ancient marks of the church are known by their Greek names—*liturgica, didache, diakonia, koinonia*, and *kerygma*.

4. Notable exceptions include the Seventh Day Adventists, whose worship life maintains the rhythm of the Jewish Shabbat.

of Christ weekly in particular congregations and mission communities that we might glorify and love our Triune God.[5]

In the Reformed tradition, community worship happens when the Word of God is preached and the sacraments are rightly administered to the people. The trouble, of course, is that as Christians we are people of the Word, shaped by the stories of God's revelation in Scripture, which is the cradle of *the living Word* Jesus Christ. While some like quoting St. Francis of Assisi's line, "share the gospel and when necessary use words," in today's postmodern and post-Christendom world sharing God's Word through proclamation is a critical gift of grace to a broken and frightened world. The Word is like that pesky mustard seed that grows wild and resists being curbed by people's distaste alone. As Karl Barth argued, "The Word cries out for belief, for this acceptance in recognition, trust, and obedience. And since faith is not an end in itself, this cry of the Word means that it demands to be proclaimed to the world to which it is directed from the outset."[6]

Praise is a natural reaction to experiencing the depth of God's love for us. Before we could ever know or love God, God knows and loves us. We are called to praise God in order to recognize the presence and transforming power of God at work in the world. Enrollment in the school of Jesus we call the church involves a reorientation of our lives to see the world through a doxological lens. Everything we do inside and outside of worship is praise. As Northern Irish musician Robin Mark said once in an interview, "There is one thing we do on earth that we will continue to do in Heaven. That is to praise and worship God. That is why we view life on earth, for those who love Jesus, as choir practice for Heaven."[7] For as important as worship is, in a culture of affluence our worship must be placed within the larger framework of Sabbath keeping, lest we fall into the trap of consumerist religion that believes a brief, weekly religious ritual is the same as obedient, joyful discipleship to the risen Christ. Indeed, regular Sunday worship set within the broader framework of Sabbath keeping could be understood in terms of an act of civil disobedience in a consumer culture.

In honor of Christ we recognize that Jesus, as a faithful Jew, practiced Shabbat. Jesus honored the commandment to rest on the seventh day of the week from sundown on Friday night to sunset the next day. This keeping of Sabbath, or the seventh day of rest, has helped Jewish people for thousands

5. Long, *Testimony,* 104.

6. Barth, *Evangelical Theology,* 37.

7. Mark, *Come Heal This Land* liner notes.

of years appreciate both the God-given function of our working lives as well as the renewal practice of resting from labor. That does not mean that people have always been faithful in keeping the Sabbath but the attempt to do so has shaped Jewish community and individual life for generation after generation. Indeed, there is an old Jewish expression that says, "The Sabbath has kept the Jews more than the Jews have kept the Sabbath." I wonder if we could say the same thing about Christians?

But Sabbath-keeping is a difficult practice of faith. Even Jesus ran into trouble trying to keep the Sabbath. Take the story that Luke tells for example:

> He was teaching in one of the meeting places on the Sabbath. There was a woman present, so twisted and bent over with arthritis that she couldn't even look up. She had been afflicted with this for eighteen years. When Jesus saw her, he called her over. "Woman, you're free!" He laid hands on her and suddenly she was standing straight and tall, giving glory to God.[8]

At first glance it is a beautiful healing story that takes place between Jesus and this crippled woman suffering almost two decades with something that we might call rheumatoid arthritis today. Oddly, she does not call out to Jesus as others do in the Gospels, nor does she reach out to touch the hem of his garment. In fact, she is not even required to recite the Apostles Creed', the Westminster Shorter Catechism, or, say, the Sinner's Prayer. No, she makes no faith statement at all—other than showing up in God's house. Jesus sees her. Jesus calls her. Jesus heals her.

And in response the clergy types say, "Praise the Lord and pass the offering plate, we've got a healing on our hands!" No, the clergy of the day are *outraged* that this upstart, undocumented rabbi from the Galilee has broken Sabbath law and performed healing in the synagogue. Luke records:

> The meeting-place president, furious because Jesus had healed on the Sabbath, said to the congregation, "Six days have been defined as work days. Come on one of the six if you want to be healed, but not on the seventh, the Sabbath."[9]

It's possible, of course, to hear the response of the clergy types in Jesus' day to Sabbath-keeping and dismiss it as pure legalism. After all, the commitment to Sabbath-keeping for many people seems like something from

8. Luke 13:10–13, *The Message.*
9. Luke 13:14, *The Message.*

a different time and place. I recall working as a research assistant at the University of Toronto and reading about ancestors in the faith from the last century who were a part of the Lord's Day Alliance Movement in Canada. The group, which appeared to be as much fun as the Women's Christian Temperance Union crowd, rallied people against street cars running on Sunday and used their significant Christendom power to put pressure on the government. It's hard now for many of us to spot how Sunday is different than any other day of the week when it comes to public transit, retail, or social media obligations. In fact, Sabbath-keeping as a societal norm I think has changed everywhere to the ends of the earth. I recall serving the Presbyterian Church in Ireland on sabbatical several years ago, and watching with curiosity as the BBC had a feature program on the Scottish Ferries beginning Sunday service for the first time ever to the remote Island of Lewis in the Hebrides. Local church groups gathered by the wharf in Stornoway, and protested the end of this last bastion of social control the Church of Scotland possessed. Dear, dear. What would John Knox do?

If Sabbath has become passé in our culture what might missional leadership do in response? For those of us who are trying to figure out what it means to follow Jesus today in the midst of a culture of affluence, how might we reframe this notion of Sabbath to be less duty orientated and more grace filled?

One place to begin is to look closer at the two traditions concerning the Sabbath. The first in Exodus 20 makes a connection with the first creation story in the book of Genesis, where God works hard for six days as a builder and then takes a day off:

> Observe the Sabbath day, to keep it holy. Work six days and do everything you need to do. But the seventh day is a Sabbath to God, your God. Don't do any work—not you, nor your son, nor your daughter, nor your servant, nor your maid, nor your animals, not even the foreign guest visiting in your town. For in six days God made Heaven, Earth, and sea, and everything in them; he rested on the seventh day. Therefore God blessed the Sabbath day; he set it apart as a holy day.[10]

The second Sabbath tradition in Deuteronomy 5 is quite different, however:

> No working on the Sabbath; keep it holy just as God, your God, commanded you. Work six days, doing everything you have to do, but the seventh day is a Sabbath, a Rest Day—no work: not

10. Exodus 20:8–11, *NRSV*.

you, your son, your daughter, your servant, your maid, your ox, your donkey (or any of your animals), and not even the foreigner visiting your town. That way your servants and maids will get the same rest as you. Don't ever forget that you were slaves in Egypt and God, your God, got you out of there in a powerful show of strength. That's why God, your God, commands you to observe the day of Sabbath rest.[11]

In Deuteronomy, the Sabbath is linked to the Exodus and the escape from Pharaoh. Creation and redemption are both needed for our human rest and re-creation. In other words, there was a clear sense that Sabbath was an expression of freedom, liberty, and justice. In the Gospels, Jesus bristled at the legalism used by some of the religious leaders that outlawed healing and other crucial works of compassion on the Sabbath. Jesus reminded the people that the Sabbath was made for humankind not humankind for the Sabbath. To understand Sabbath legalistically was to become a slave once more—this time to a day of the week instead of an Egyptian taskmaster. Jesus reacted this way in the Gospel:

> But Jesus shot back, "You frauds! Each Sabbath every one of you regularly unties your cow or donkey from its stall, leads it out for water, and thinks nothing of it. So why isn't it all right for me to untie this daughter of Abraham and lead her from the stall where Satan has had her tied these eighteen years?" When he put it that way, his critics were left looking quite silly and red-faced. The congregation was delighted and cheered him on.[12]

Jesus says it's ridiculous not to heal the woman, after all by the law a bound animal, a tied up donkey, is unbound, set free on the Sabbath to drink. Why would he not heal this child of God, this daughter of Abraham, who has been bound not for a day but for eighteen years? It's hard to argue with that.

This is not Sabbath-keeping as duty, but rather as pure gift, what we call in the school of Jesus grace. This understanding of Sabbath as gift and not duty flourished after Jesus' resurrection, when followers of the risen Lord gathered on Sundays (resurrection day) for a meal, worship, and fellowship. This was not a day off, however, and most would simply gather together after work. Friday at sundown until Saturday evening remained the Jewish Sabbath and many Jewish Christians observed both the traditional Sabbath and the Sunday worship celebration called "the Lord's Day." As

11. Deuteronomy 5:12–15, *NRSV.*

12. Luke 13:15–17, *The Message.*

more and more Gentiles joined the Christian church, however, the practice of attending both the Jewish Sabbath and the Christian Sunday service decreased. Finally, in 321 AD Roman Emperor Constantine made Sunday the official day of rest, and Christians effectively collapsed the Sabbath in with "the Lord's Day." For Christians, the day of resurrection, God's grace-filled response to human greed and sin, is combined with the day of freedom rooted deeply in our Jewish past.

How do we practice Sabbath as individuals as well as a church? How do we support one another in keeping Sabbath?

Theologian Dorothy Bass suggests that Christians should be focused on taking a rest from work, commerce, and worry. According to Bass resting from work helps us value the work we do the other six days of the week, and provides a space for our relationship with God as well as family and friends to grow. Sabbath is also a rest from commerce. Whenever possible it frees us from the rat race of buying and consuming and frees us from the need to always be focused on material possessions. And worry? It is not always possible to put worries out of our minds but refraining from paying bills, preparing tax returns, and making lists of things to do in the week to come will cut down on Sabbath worries.

Marva Dawn also offers direction to those who seek to practice Sabbath in her work *Keeping the Sabbath Wholly*. Dawn invites Christians to engage four practices on the Sabbath—ceasing, resting, embracing, and feasting. Dawn also desires to reclaim the Jewish roots of Sabbath, noting that as a Christian she thinks of Sabbath not as all day Sunday but as beginning at sundown Saturday night to sundown on Sunday. In other words, getting together with friends for a great dinner party with a fine bottle of wine on Saturday night is the start of Sabbath. Sunday worship and a restful afternoon is also Sabbath. Checking emails by 8 PM on Sunday and getting one's head into the workplace for Monday morning is not a betrayal of Sabbath, but rather it is simply an acknowledgement that for many working people Sunday night is not restful.

To illustrate the importance of Sabbath, Dawn tells the story of a group of settlers who set out from St. Louis bound for Oregon to set up a new settlement here in the West. They were faithful Christian disciples who traveled hard six days a week but stopped to keep Sabbath on the seventh day. As their journey dragged on, however, many in the group feared they would not reach the West Coast before winter and an argument began about whether they should skip the Sabbath and just push on. The group decided that they would split in two—one group would maintain the Sabbath rest, the other would travel seven days a week. The group continued to travel together for that week and when the Sabbath came they divided, leaving the Sabbath-keeping group behind. Can you guess what happened? The group of settlers and pioneers who arrived first on the West Coast were Sabbath keepers and not the group that pushed themselves seven days a week. The Sabbath keepers, and their horses, actually traveled farther and faster by taking a day to cease, rest, embrace, and feast to the glory of God.

In a culture of affluence, in a never ending "keeping up with the Joneses," it is easy to feel like that woman hunched over in pain in the synagogue, overwhelmed with the burdens of contemporary life. The commitment to Sabbath keeping as a practice of discipleship offers each and every person the promise of that same freedom that Christ still gives those who seek him with an open heart.

STUDY

If, as disciples, we have come through a Holy Spirit-led process of discovery regarding, "Who am I?" "Who is Jesus?" and "Who am I *in* Jesus?" then it comes as no surprise that enrollment in the school of Jesus we call the church includes a deep commitment to study. Disciple, or *Talmid* (*Talmadim* plural) in Hebrew or Mathetes in Greek, means a learner or pupil of the master or rabbi. Therefore, we are students of Rabbi Jesus and we dedicate our lives to *didache*, or studying and practicing what our rabbi has taught us.

A working definition of a missionary disciple's study includes *a commitment to regular study of Scripture; a desire to be "transformed by the renewing of the mind"*;[13] *and a curiosity to engage contemporary issues and challenges through "faith seeking understanding."*

We've already touched on the Apostle Paul's teaching from Romans:

> Therefore, I urge you, brothers and sisters, in view of God's mercy, to offer your bodies as a living sacrifice, holy and pleasing to God—this is your true and proper worship. Do not conform to the pattern of this world, but be transformed by the renewing of your mind. Then you will be able to test and approve what God's will is—his good, pleasing and perfect will.[14]

13. Romans 12:2, *NIV.*
14. Romans 12:1–2, *NIV.*

Paul knows firsthand what it means to be transformed by the renewing of his mind. Christ himself, the headmaster, showed up in a dramatic way to teach Paul the unforced rhythms of God's grace. Paul, a persecutor of the Christian movement, was transformed from Saul to Paul on the Damascus Road where he "came to life" through a real-life encounter with the risen Jesus. As a result, Paul became arguably the best-known thinker, preacher, and evangelist of the early church movement. Today in North America we name everything from churches and cities to hockey arenas and hospitals after him. While himself a faithful Jew, Paul advanced the bold argument that what God did in Jesus was for all people in the world. Through being yoked to Christ, he learned that a crucified Jew now ruled the cosmos. Paul set about the known world, the Roman Empire at the time, spreading the gospel of Jesus Christ. He preached that people were enslaved, like zombies, to sin, and that through the life, death, and resurrection of Jesus we are set free to be truly human, fully alive, beloved children of God. And that once we've been freed who would want to go back to slavery, to a zombie-like state. As the Gospel of John proclaims, "So if the Son sets you free, you will be free indeed."[15]

Paul, ever the scholar, ever the thinker, sits down to write one of many, many letters of encouragement to the little churches scattered through the Roman Empire. Now the arrival of the letter we call the book of Romans, written by Paul in the city of Corinth likely in the autumn of 57 AD, would not have caused any fanfare in the imperial capital. After all, Rome was the center of power, a place where correspondence was received daily on all matters of importance. And Paul's letter would not have gone to the wealthy or powerful citizens of Roman living up on one of the seven hills surrounding the city. No, scholars suggest that the early Christians living in Rome were the working poor, down by the riverbank, clustered in little house churches. It is here that the letter to the Romans arrives.

What's ironic is of all the important documents to arrive in Rome that day at the Imperial Senate, or poetry shared in famous halls of learning and philosophy, it is this letter that lives on down through the ages. In fact, Paul's Letter to Romans could be said to be the most important of the all the letters in the New Testament. It helped shape the theology of the Reformation and our church. Paul sets out, ever the thinker, ever the scholar, to make sense of what God did in the world, to the world, and for the world through Jesus.

15. John 8:36, *NIV.*

When you read the Letter to the Romans you'll find a sophisticated theological review of God's activity in the world, especially through the covenant with Israel. Paul is very, very clear that God has not given up on Israel, but rather through Israel has invited the world in. As one cheeky translator once said, "When Israel walked out on God in the crucifixion of Jesus, they left the door wide open for the rest of the world to walk in." I like that.

In fact, Paul goes to great lengths to make it clear that Israel is still in God's favor, and that all are welcome in the community of Christ. Freed from sin, freed from that zombie-like state, Paul says, "Therefore. . ." beginning this passage. Read it in full:

> So here's what I want you to do, God helping you: Take your everyday, ordinary life—your sleeping, eating, going-to-work, and walking-around life—and place it before God as an offering. Embracing what God does for you is the best thing you can do for him. Don't become so well-adjusted to your culture that you fit into it without even thinking. Instead, fix your attention on God. You'll be changed from the inside out. Readily recognize what he wants from you, and quickly respond to it. Unlike the culture around you, always dragging you down to its level of immaturity, God brings the best out of you, develops well-formed maturity in you.
>
> I'm speaking to you out of deep gratitude for all that God has given me, and especially as I have responsibilities in relation to you. Living then, as every one of you does, in pure grace, it's important that you not misinterpret yourselves as people who are bringing this goodness to God. No, God brings it all to you. The only accurate way to understand ourselves is by what God is and by what he does for us, not by what we are and what we do for him.
>
> In this way we are like the various parts of a human body. Each part gets its meaning from the body as a whole, not the other way around. The body we're talking about is Christ's body of chosen people. Each of us finds our meaning and function as a part of his body. But as a chopped-off finger or cut-off toe we wouldn't amount to much, would we? So since we find ourselves fashioned into all these excellently formed and marvelously functioning parts in Christ's body, let's just go ahead and be what we were made to be, without enviously or pridefully comparing ourselves with each other, or trying to be something we aren't.

> If you preach, just preach God's Message, nothing else; if you help,
> just help, don't take over; if you teach, stick to your teaching; if you
> give encouraging guidance, be careful that you don't get bossy; if
> you're put in charge, don't manipulate; if you're called to give aid
> to people in distress, keep your eyes open and be quick to respond;
> if you work with the disadvantaged, don't let yourself get irritated
> with them or depressed by them. Keep a smile on your face.[16]

As disciples we learn that we are set free by God to be fully human and fully alive. Therefore, as early pupils in the school of Jesus we call the church, we study closely three things that the Holy Spirit teaches through Paul's writing.

First, disciples are to offer our lives as a living sacrifice for God. What does that mean? Many ancient religions offered sacrifices, but they were killed as part of the ritual. Paul says we are *living* sacrifices, our lives are to put to good and faithful use. Parents often have an intuitive sense of being a living sacrifice. From getting up early to drive to hockey practice or standing in the pouring November rain coaching a soccer team—a living sacrifice. From forgoing that new set of golf clubs so your daughter can have braces to not taking that promotion at work so the family can stay in the place they love—a living sacrifice. From diapers to paying for diplomas or a down payment on a child's first home—a living sacrifice. For all of us, parents or not, we know something of a living sacrifice. It is any action that requires selflessness, that Holy Spirit-fueled action of overcoming our selfish sins, in order to be Christ for another person. A living sacrifice. As we study this teaching of Paul further he makes a second point.

Not only are our lives as Christians to be marked by active sacrifice, choosing others over ourselves, but we are also called to dedicate our *minds* as well as our bodies to honor God. Do not conform to this world. Be transformed by the renewing of your mind. As missional leaders in a culture of affluence, God equips us to bring a theological lens to bear on the world, and those tinted glasses help us to see things differently. I remember many years ago taking my youth group from an affluent neighborhood in Toronto to a big youth revival weekend north of the city. The teens had an amazing time with the Christian rap music, dry ice, lasers, and all the other stereotypes that go with an event of that kind. The theme was "Be transformed by the renewing of your mind." It was the year the Hollywood blockbuster *The Matrix* was released and the organizers played clips of the movie to connect

16. Romans 12:1–8, *The Message*.

with Paul's teaching in Romans. The movie is about a computer programmer named Neo who discovers that reality as he knows it is all a lie, and that reality is much different and darker than he had been raised to believe. The movie is laced with biblical imagery—the free humans live in a place called Zion, a main character is called Trinity, and so forth. Once Neo is given a glimpse of reality, he is also given a choice by the mysterious character Morpheus. Morpheus tells Neo that he has been born into slavery—bondage of the mind. Morpheus gives Neo a choice. He can take one colored pill and return to a state of ignorance or he can take a different colored pill and live with this new knowledge and fight for the truth in a world full of lies and deception. Needless to say, the teens loved the connection. It was probably one of the best times for small group theological discussion as we dug into what Paul meant when he said, "do not conform to this world but be transformed by the renewing of your mind." As missionary disciples, our sanctified imagination is employed in a lifelong act of resistance against a dominant culture that attempts to mask the kingdom reality present in God's creation.

Our discussion led into Paul's third point in the passage—discover the gifts that God has given to each of us and use them for the sake of his glory. The ability to do all these things, to live sacrificially instead of selfishly, to not live by the world's values but to focus on the will of God in Jesus Christ, to discern one's unique God-given gifts and not boast about them using them instead to the glory of God, comes as a gift of the Holy Spirit. Much of this is revealed over time through careful study and learning as a disciple enrolled in the school of Jesus we call the church. If we know anything of God, it is because God has revealed something of himself to us, but that does not mean as human creatures we are simply passive. I'll be over here God, and if you want to tell me something important that would be great. God did not hard wire us as human creatures to be that way. We are curious, we are motivated by wonder, we are called to explore the farthest reaches of this world and this galaxy, and we are called to explore the furthest reaches of our mind through imagination. Our commitment to study, both God's Word and God's world, is a key mark of people, freed from sin, and set free to live for the glory of God. John Calvin once said, "True wisdom consists of two things: knowledge of God and knowledge of ourselves."[17] This desire to know more about God and humanity is at the heart of theological study. Theology is, in the classic definition, "Faith, seeking understanding." A life

17. Calvin, *Institutes of the Christian Religion,* 1.1.1.

of discipleship rooted in faithful study prepares us to witness in a world where people often nurse an anemic agnosticism.

People often carry a misshapen understanding of the Divine, like the businessperson I met on a recent flight. I sat down beside a man and said hello, chatting a bit while I fumbled with my earphones for the in-flight entertainment. We talked a bit about what part of Vancouver he lived in, his hobbies, and his kids. Then, just as the safety video was finishing, we finally got around to the inevitable work question. He was in the mining industry, in some executive role. Then he asked me, "So what do you do for work?" "Well," I said, "I'm a pastor."

"Oh, well, I don't believe in God," he said dismissively. Often when people say that they assume they are shutting down a conversation when it is possible the real conversation is just beginning. I said in reply, "Hmm, tell me about the God you *don't* believe in." Well, the businessperson starting talking about his childhood and his disappointment with the church, his image of a vengeful, angry God who sits on the clouds with a beard and zaps people with lightning bolts. The man talked and talked so long that the fasten seat belt sign was off and the drink trolley was part way down the aisle by the time he finished. As is so often the case when I ask that question I casually replied at the end, "Well, I don't believe in that god either. Let me tell you about Jesus." A lifetime of study as a disciple prepares us for the conversations that matter and enables us to go deeper with God and other human beings.

STEWARDSHIP

Another ancient mark of the church was koinonia, unfortunately often translated to the rather fussy "Grandma's parlor" language of fellowship with the inevitable connotation of store-bought cookies and weak coffee. Fellowship or koinonia really speaks of community and belonging. It might seem odd, therefore, to link the language of stewardship, most often associated with money, to the concept of koinonia. I want to knit the two together, however, because in a culture of affluence how we spend our money says a lot about what we value, and where we long to belong. The right car, clothes, and club membership say a lot through our finances about where, and by whom, we want to be accepted and approved. Of course, stewardship is more than money. A working definition of stewardship for a missionary disciple would include *a commitment to live generously in Christian community trusting that "The Lord loves a cheerful giver";*[18] *a desire to share the time, talent and treasure God has granted us in abundance, a curiosity to explore what it means to be "rich toward God"*[19] *by living by the rule, "Earn all you can, save all you can, give all you can."*[20]

Acts 2 is often cited as a vision of what Christian community should look like:

> They devoted themselves to the apostles' teaching and to fellowship, to the breaking of bread and to prayer. Everyone was filled with awe at the many wonders and signs performed by the apostles. All the believers were together and had everything in common. They sold property and possessions to give to anyone who had need. Every day they continued to meet together in the temple courts. They broke bread in their homes and ate together with glad and sincere hearts, praising God and enjoying the favor of all the people. And the Lord added to their number daily those who were being saved.[21]

It is clear in this vision of the early church stewardship and fellowship go hand in hand. This is not a church that encourages people to live separate, private lives six days a week with a drive in commute to "consume a worship experience" one morning a week. No, this is a mission community that is taking seriously that, if Jesus is Lord of our whole lives, we must share everything with those around us. From Acts 2 we see that when stewardship and fellowship are united, hospitality to others becomes a key mark of the mission community. As Alan Hirsch says, "hospitality is an expression and experience of God's character," and a commitment to "creating an environment where people in their local community experience the character of God, feel a sense of belonging before believing, and can explore their spirituality with freedom."[22]

Like Sarah and Abraham by the oaks of the Mamre, mission communities need to be filled with an expectation of revelation in their midst and ready to respond when God shows up.[23] In her work *Christianity for*

18. 2 Corinthians 9:7, *NIV.*

19. Luke 12:21, *NIV.*

20. Wesley, "Sermon on the Use of Money," in Outler and Heitzenrater, eds., *John Wesley's Sermons,* 355.

21. Acts 2:42–47, *NIV.*

22. Hirsch and Altclass, *Forgotten Ways Handbook,* 105.

23. Genesis 18:1–15.

the Rest of Us, Diana Butler Bass names *hospitality* as the first key Christian practice that thriving mainline Protestant congregations are engaging as they buck the trend and journey back from denominational decline. Draw-ing on Henri Nouwen's teaching, Bass suggests that congregations practice hospitality "not to change people, but to offer them space where change can take place."[24] Abraham and Sarah's eagerness to practice hospitality to strangers reflects our faith tradition's understanding that by doing so we both entertain angels unaware as well as encounter Christ who said, "I was hungry and you gave me food, I was thirsty and you gave me something to drink, I was a stranger and you welcomed me, I was naked and you gave me clothing, I was sick and you took care of me, I was in prison and you visited me."[25] In fact, John Bowen concludes that the community of faith's hospitality is the oldest mark of evangelism in Scripture. As Bowen argues

> God's intention in calling Abraham is not to shower blessings on one favorite child and turn away from the rest. God's desire is to bless the whole world. God is not the parent who says to one child, "You're the only one I'm going to give an allowance to because I like you best." Rather, God is the parent who says, "Here, you take this week's allowance and share it with your sisters and brothers." The blessing is for all. . . . God's intention is that others will look at Abraham's people and say in effect, "Boy, those people really know how to live. Look at how they care for one another. See how they take care of people with disabilities? What makes them that way? They say it's something to do with their religion. Maybe we'd better check it out."[26]

Hospitality is not simply "being friendly." Where stewardship and fellow-ship unite, there is potential for selfless living for the sake of the other—a sign of God's agape love in the world. As Bryan Stone argues, if the effective witness of a community can be "measured" at all it can best be measured by "how well a community prepares a place at its table for those who are not there yet, for those who have not even heard, much less heeded, its invitation."[27]

In an attempt to make hospitality a priority, it becomes clear that mission communities must help disciples to understand the shift from

24. Bass, *Christianity,* 79.
25. Hebrews 13:2 and Matthew 25:35–36, *NRSV.*
26. Bowen, *Evangelism for Normal People,* 29–31.
27. Stone, *Evangelism after Christendom,* 274.

modernism to postmodernism and how that affects congregational ministry. In *The Gospel According to Starbucks* Leonard Sweet argues that the church historically has served as a "third place" for community experiences between work and home. Sweet defines a third place in the following way:

- It is neutral ground.

- It is inclusive and promotes social equality

- Conversation is the central activity.

- It is frequented by regulars who welcome newcomers.

- It is typically in a non-pretentious, homey place.

- It fosters a playful mood.[28]

Clearly, in previous generations the church was that third place to gather for social events, sporting activities, meals, service opportunities, and religious ritual. Sweet suggests that in the last century the church slowly moved away from its role as the third place when

> churches increasingly became not relational space but propositional place. Instead of going there to connect with God and with others in meaningful relationship, people started going to church to be convinced of transcendent truth, or, if they already numbered among the convinced, to have their beliefs and religious convictions confirmed from the pulpit. The church lost credibility as a place for sacred relationship when it chose to specialize in formulating and advancing a better spiritual argument. The result is that people who came to the meeting house got connected with ideas and formulas than they did with God and with other people.[29]

I struggle with Sweet's clear-cut, black-and-white take on relational versus propositional place. Surely, the classic understanding of theology as "*fides quarens intellectum*" or "faith seeking understanding" resists this reductionist approach that Sweet proposes. There are plenty of "relational" spaces that are not transformative and not to be admired. An alcoholic, for example, can find a relational third space in a local bar but the relational third space where transformation happens is the Alcoholics Anonymous meeting down the street in the church basement. Nevertheless, it is fascinating that despite the rapid decline of the church in Canada as the third place,

28. Sweet, *Gospel According to Starbucks,* 132.

29. Ibid.

faith in God amongst the general population remains high. Reginald Bibby, Canada's leading sociologist of religion, reports that at a time when only 20 percent of Canadians say they attend religious services just about every week, some 80 percent of Canadian adults and teenagers assert positive belief in God. Furthermore, this strong belief in God has remained virtually the same since 1975, despite the fact that attendance at religious services dropped between 1975 and 2000 from about 30 percent of the population to 20 percent.[30]

In effect, the human need for community, or what we might call fellowship, is still being met but in a new third place outside of church from coffee shops to yoga classes to the local pub. Of course, these third places are not benign or without moral values of their own. As Bryan Stone reminds us, we live in a "culture of conversion" where in "every direction we turn, we are offered the promise of 'makeover,' whether of body, face, wardrobe, career, marriage, home, personality, or soul."[31] Driven primarily by the powerful, quasi-religious influence of consumerism, these new third places exercise considerable control and influence over the population that serves as a formidable challenge to the gospel. As Stone concludes

> To be converted is not something strange or out of the ordinary in our world. It is roughly equivalent to the air we breathe. In fact, part of what makes the call to Christian conversion strike us as so radical and invasive today is the level to which we have become acclimated to our ongoing conversion and formation by a staggering range of powers that contradict Christian faith and community and serve ends other than the shalom of God's reign.[32]

Rather than trying to convert the dominant culture to the gospel, missional leadership today has a high degree of comfort with being countercultural, using our sanctified imagination for the new world that God is shaping. Therefore, the norms around stewardship and fellowship within a mission community will look and feel very different from other communities. Every family has rules that the members of that body are expected to abide by. The rules govern the health and vitality of their common life together. Be home by 11 PM. Put out the garbage on Wednesday mornings. Don't forget to lock the door when you leave the house. Leave the toilet seat down. And so forth.

30. Bibby, *Restless Churches*, 14–15.
31. Stone, *Evangelism after Christendom*, 258.
32. Ibid.

Some mission communities call these norms their "Rule of Life," but whatever you refer to them as they directly affect the nature of fellowship or community life together as Christians. One Mission Community I belonged to developed the following guidelines for life together:

Mission: Rooted in love of God and neighbor and guided by the Holy Spirit, *we are called to help make disciples for Jesus*, who will bless and mend God's broken and beloved world.[33]

Vision: God the Holy Trinity calls us to be compassionate to all people and to live and love as Jesus has taught us. Together we will continue to build a nurturing and vibrant Christian community that enhances God's reputation in the world through our commitment to follow Jesus through the Great Commandment and the Great Commission.[34]

Values: Seeking to honor God and to live by goodness and mercy all the days of our lives, as a Christian community we value:[35]

Love—as God's gift to us through the cross of Christ and through the forgiveness of sin to be shared generously and joyfully with the world.

Scripture—as the primary source of authority and revelation and as a witness to the Risen Christ and the ongoing work of the Holy Spirit. The witness of the Old and New Testament, while primary, are interpreted by reason, tradition, and experience, converted by the Holy Spirit.

Relationships—as a bond of deep affection and a sign of covenant with the Triune God, one another and the world. Our stewardship of time, talent, and treasure within community reflects our trust in both who and whose we are.

Worship—as the core expression of what it means to be fully human as a means of knowing God and enjoying God forever.

Diversity—as a sign of God's blessing and trust that the body of Christ is made stronger by the contribution of all.[36]

---

33. Ephesians 3:17, Mark 12:29–31.
34. Matthew 22:36–40, Matthew 28:18–20.
35. Psalm 23.
36. Galatians 3:28.

Evangelism—as a means of knowing Christ and making Him known while sharing the "Hope that is within us"[37] and helping others take steps towards faith in Jesus.

Justice—as a faithful way to respond to God's activity in the world through ethical and prophetic vision that helps us honor the Trinity by "seeking justice, loving kindness and walking humbly with our God."[38]

Knowing the rules that we live by helps build our common life together. It comes as no surprise then that stewardship and fellowship go hand in hand, since one cannot truly exist without the other. Martin Luther is rumored to have once said; "God put fingers on our hand for the money to slide through them so He can give us more. Whatever a person gives away, God will reimburse." It is unmistakable how often Jesus comments on stewardship regarding wealth and possessions in the gospels. As Rouse and Van Gelder note

> Sixteen of Jesus' thirty-eight parables are concerned with money and possessions. An amazing one out of ten verses in the Gospels (288 in all) deal directly with the subject of money. The Bible offers 500 verses on prayer, fewer than 500 verses on faith, yet more than 2,000 verses on money and possessions. It seems that Jesus realized that one's attitude toward possessions was indeed a spiritual matter and needed to be taken seriously.[39]

This invitation to live in Christian community with a generous spirit is at the heart of that beautiful vision of the early church sharing all in common in the book of Acts. What is fascinating is that just three short chapters later we are given a clear example of what happens to the fellowship of the church when selfishness rather than selflessness corrupts stewardship. In a rather colorful story Luke tells the story of where a toxic mix of country club religion and selfish stewardship cause death:

> But a man named Ananias—his wife, Sapphira, conniving in this with him—sold a piece of land, secretly kept part of the price for himself, and then brought the rest to the apostles and made an offering of it. Peter said, "Ananias, how did Satan get you to lie to

37. 1 Peter 3:15.

38. Micah 6:8.

39. Rouse and Van Gelder, *Field Guide*, 114–15.

the Holy Spirit and secretly keep back part of the price of the field? Before you sold it, it was all yours, and after you sold it, the money was yours to do with as you wished. So what got into you to pull a trick like this? You didn't lie to men but to God." Ananias, when he heard those words, fell down dead. That put the fear of God into everyone who heard of it. The younger men went right to work and wrapped him up, then carried him out and buried him. Not more than three hours later, his wife, knowing nothing of what had happened, came in. Peter said, "Tell me, were you given this price for your field?" "Yes," she said, "that price." Peter responded, "What's going on here that you connived to conspire against the Spirit of the Master? The men who buried your husband are at the door, and you're next." No sooner were the words out of his mouth than she also fell down, dead. When the young men returned they found her body. They carried her out and buried her beside her husband. By this time the whole church and, in fact, everyone who heard of these things had a healthy respect for God. They knew God was not to be trifled with.[40]

Imagine the parking lot conversation after that church meeting. Wow. As students enrolled in the school of Jesus we call the church, it is important to practice stewardship tied to fellowship so that we may live lives that give evidence of being generous saints.

I will always remember a pre-sermon illustration used at Trinity United Church of Christ in south Chicago many years ago. Otis Moss III set up two tables at the front of the sanctuary. He had deacons bring up grocery bags full of ten different kinds of items like apples and bananas. In an illustration of tithing, he invited the deacons to place nine items on one table and one on the other. After several deacons came forward the table receiving nine items was overflowing and the one receiving just one looked bare. Moss said, "This table only receiving one item is what we are asked by the Bible to give to God. Look at our table, it's overflowing with abundance. And yet, we say, 'Oh, I can't give ten percent to God—what will I live on.' God wants us to be generous. God needs us to be generous. For the sake of the world he died to save."

As disciples our stewardship is yoked to our fellowship with other Christians for the sake of the world God died to save. As Martin Luther said to his family while dying, "I have nothing [in worldly goods] to bequest to you, but I have a rich God. Him I leave to you. He will nourish you well."

40. Acts 5:1–11, *The Message.*

SERVICE

The Christian practice of service is rooted deeply in a sense of participating in God's mission in the world. The ancient description of service as *diakonia* emerges in the reality of the early church trying to live out a resurrected life and while both partnering with and modeling the revealed agape love found in Father, Son, and Holy Spirit. The book of Acts records

> During this time, as the disciples were increasing in numbers by leaps and bounds, hard feelings developed among the Greek-speaking believers—"Hellenists"—toward the Hebrew-speaking believers because their widows were being discriminated against in the daily food lines. So the Twelve called a meeting of the disciples. They said, "It wouldn't be right for us to abandon our responsibilities for preaching and teaching the Word of God to help with the care of the poor. So, friends, choose seven men from among you whom everyone trusts, men full of the Holy Spirit and good sense, and we'll assign them this task. Meanwhile, we'll stick to our assigned tasks of prayer and speaking God's Word." The congregation thought this was a great idea. They went ahead and chose—Stephen, a man full of faith and the Holy Spirit, Philip, Procorus, Nicanor, Timon, Parmenas, Nicolas, a convert from Antioch. Then they presented them to the apostles. Praying, the apostles laid on hands and commissioned them for their task.[41]

Mission, John Bowen argues, means love. Showing God's love in the world through serving others is an acknowledgement that we are partnering with the mission of God that is "a shorthand of saying that God's love is at work in the world, putting right everything that is wrong—sin and evil and suffering—and restoring joy and wholeness to the world."[42] Therefore, service includes *a commitment to love and serve others through acts of compassion and caring while seeking justice that changes lives for good; a desire to be a "good and faithful servant";*[43] *a curiosity to explore your God-given gifts by partnering with the Holy Spirit and discovering where God is already at work reconciling the world around us.*

Missional leadership does not view "service" as one more "to do" action on a busy list but rather an opportunity to join with what God is up to in the neighborhood around us. Some people describe service in and

41. Acts 6:1–6, *The Message.*

42. Bowen, ed., *Green Shoots,* 3.

43. Matthew 25:23.

through the church that, stripped away, sounds a lot like charity that is human agency driven. Missional theology imagines service more like riding a bicycle made for two. At first you may get the impression that the movement and experience are of our own doing but pretty soon you discover that there is another power, presence, and person sharing the ride and directing the action. Missional service invites us to become, in the words of Allan Roxburgh, "detectives of divinity" with an expectation of revelation in the world asking, "What is God up to, out ahead of us in the neighborhoods and communities where we live?"[44]

Living out our calling as missionary disciples through service to God's World helps since it "eschews preferences for comfort, style, and denominational branding and invites us to look outward to where the Missio Dei is at work among the poor, the marginalized, the lost and the beleaguered."[45] Trusting deeply that our fragile, fallible human lives can, by the power of the Holy Spirit, reflect the mutual, self-giving love revealed at the heart of God, Father, Son, and Holy Spirit, we engage in service to the world understanding that even the smallest action is participating in the reconciling work of the kingdom that is here and is coming. Frost encourages that service to God through neighbor when he writes,

> Truly incarnational Christians live in the neighborhoods where they're serving God. They are deeply concerned about partnering with the unfurling of God's kingdom so they do know who lives there and what cultural and social expressions are present. They take the idea of place very seriously. I've heard it said that place is just a space that has a narrative history. The job of the missional community is to learn that history to retell it in a redemptive way.[46]

Missional leadership in a culture of affluence clarifies that service to God's world is not a token "hit-and-run" charity act that makes us "feel good" like a bun toss in a poor neighborhood on a Saturday morning, with privileged teenagers from the suburbs in tow. No, missional service is the risky business of entering fully into the lives of those around us with the trust that the incarnational Triune God is already out ahead of us creating opportunities for us to put "love in action" and witnesses that same love in friend and stranger. For years now, I have begun most days with a run through my local neighborhood. As I wake up and listen to praise music on my iPod, I

44. Bowen, ed., *Green Shoots*, 188 and 193.

45. Frost, *Road to Missional*, 71.

46. Ibid., 136.

pray for those in my neighborhood and invoke the missional mindfulness of St. Patrick, who lived and ministered in a pre-Christian society with the trust that God in Christ was clearly at work. May our missional service to God's world begin each day with this confidence:

> Christ be with me, Christ within me.
> Christ behind me, Christ before me.
> Christ beside me, Christ to win me.
> Christ to comfort and restore me.
>
> Christ beneath me, Christ above me.
> Christ in quiet, Christ in danger.
> Christ in hearts of those who love me.
> Christ in mouth of friend and stranger.

SANCTIFICATION

The fifth mark of Christian discipleship to be experienced and experimented with in the school of Jesus we call the church is sanctification. Sanctification is a fancy word meaning "to become holy" and describes our growth in holiness. While discipleship often feels like two steps forward, one step back due to the power of sin at work in the world (and us), we trust through the power of the cross and the promise of God's ultimate victory over sin and death that is possible to grow in holiness as we pattern our lives more and more after Christ. After all, David Bosch argues, "the life and work of the Christian community are intimately bound up with God's cosmic-historical plan for the redemption of the world."[47]

Therefore, a missionary disciple might define his or her lifestyle focused on sanctification *as a commitment to be filled with the Holy Spirit in order to grow into the full measure of Christ; a desire to grow in holiness and to bless and mend God's broken world through acts of grace and proclamation; and a curiosity to discern and join in God's saving and reconciling work in the neighborhood and around the world.*

While we affirm that God in Christ meets us with love and forgiveness, accepting us just as we are, we also trust that God in Christ has no intention of leaving us as God found us. Made in the image of God, we are called to grow in God's likeness. This maturing in faith and eagerness to do good in the world is a process nurtured by the Holy Spirit from baptism to

47. Bosch, *Transforming Mission, 178.*

life's end through the desire to attain the whole measure of the fullness of Christ.

I've yoked sanctification with the ancient mark of the church kerygma or the apostolic proclamation of salvation through Jesus Christ. This may seem strange to some, as kerygma often is paired with liturgica as people see proclamation as something that happens exclusively within a Sunday worship context. While the preaching of the Word in Christian worship is essential, I am placing kerygma here with the strong belief that in a post-Christendom context of North American affluence, missional leaders must recognize that our strongest witness and proclamation of the gospel is in our words and works throughout the week through relationships with others, in a culture obsessed with individualism and consumerism. Sanctification, not only as individual disciples but whole mission communities, has a profound influence on the neighborhoods where we live, work, and play. As Rick Rouse and Craig Van Gelder remind us, "It is the Spirit of God who leads congregations into sanctified living" and they are "to live consistent with their new nature" given by the Spirit so that "they might participate more fully in God's mission in the world."[48] Rouse and Van Gelder push sanctified living for the people of God further by arguing:

> We find in Galatians that living by the Spirit and being guided by the Spirit are to be the marks of the church (Gal. 5:25). In light of the new nature we have been given, we are now free to experience and express the fruits of the Spirit: love, joy, peace, patience, kindness, generosity, faithfulness, gentleness and self-control (vv. 22–23). Clearly the communities of reconciled diversity that the Spirit creates now have not only the responsibility but also the power to live by a different set of values in the world. It is this communal lifestyle that displays contrasting values to those of the world, where this lifestyle serves as the basis for the church having an effective witness in the world.[49]

This effective witness in the world, this sign of our sanctification is a little bit like a show home for the kingdom of God.

Years ago, I preached regularly at a little church north of Toronto, around Canada's Wonderland. At the time, farmer's fields that surrounded the theme park were being transformed into cookie-cutter subdivisions. From Highway 400, motorists glimpsed large advertisements of this future

48. Rouse and Van Gelder, *Field Guide*, 38.

49. Ibid.

community. The signs, complete with architect's drawings of nuclear families playing on quiet cul de sacs, were a stark contrast to the muddy fields beside the busy highway. Clearly, there was much work still to be done in order to bring this imagined future to life. The only other hint of the new creation was found in the corner of the development—a model home. One day on my way to a church meeting, I pulled off the highway and went inside to check out the show home. Taking my muddy boots off at the door, I entered a totally different reality than the fallow fields nudging the outside of the wee house. A company representative greeted me warmly with a firm handshake and an offer of a short tour. Sparkling stainless steel appliances gave way to an opportunity to warm my hands by the high-end gas fireplace in a tasteful, spacious living room. As I sank into a ridiculously plush leather couch, my eye was drawn to a nearby window and the muddy, uncultivated field beyond. As if reading my mind, the sales representative pointed past the glass pane and said, "It's a little hard to picture how one day soon all of this will be different. Hopefully this glimpse inside the show home is enough to tease your imagination."

The sales representative's line was still ringing in my head a few minutes later when I pulled into the gravel parking lot outside the little nineteenth-century church. I wondered whether our local congregations and mission communities might just be show homes of God's future development plans we call the kingdom of God. Could it be that when people enter our churches they catch just a glimpse of what God in Christ is doing to redeem the world? Is there evidence of Christ's change within us, and our worshipping communities, so powerful that is visible to pre-Christians around us? What if the way we treated each other as sisters and brothers in Christ was so different than the world outside that people were curious enough to want to find out more about who Jesus is for us . . . and for them? If our show homes were patterned appropriately to give just a glimpse of God's plan for this world and mirrored just enough of that mutual, self-giving love revealed in Father, Son, and Holy Spirit, how might that change a sin-sick and cynical world? Might our common life together be a bold announcement of God's "Kingdom Acres"—that is and is to come by God's own sovereign hand? Kingdom Acres—coming soon.

As we experience God's sanctification in our individual and common life, we model for the world around us a powerful witness to the gospel. Lives changed for good by the King of kings and Lord of lords. We model through changed lives, growing in holiness, a "show home" model of how followers of Jesus can pray, talk, and discern God's will together with gentleness and respect. By being careful not only of our behavior but also demonstrating a strong desire to avoid drawing "lines in the sand" on various political issues, missional leaders help form sanctifying communities that have a keen awareness of St. Augustine's classic statement that on "Essentials: unity. Non-essentials: liberty. All things: Charity."

Our sanctified kerygma declares, "The kingdom of God is like a show home in a muddy farmer's field. And it is marvelous in our sight. . ."

Chapter Nine

Missional Microwave
Holy Spirit Lessons on Heating Up
Lukewarm Leadership

"Set yourself on fire and people will come from miles away to watch you burn."

—John Wesley

While there is considerable hand-wringing within denominational offices these days over the state of the church, missional leaders are confident that God's Holy Spirit is out in front of us at work in the world, inviting us to partner in mission where we live, work, and play. As Mark Twain once said, "Reports of my death have been greatly exaggerated." The decline and expectant death of the church have filled countless bookcases over the last several decades and preoccupied a good deal of church leadership struggling to hold or stem the flow of people from the pews. "Seeker-sensitive" or "alternative" worship worked hard to translate the gospel into contemporary meaning but often did so with a consumerist or attractional model of ecclesiology. Marketing and mission are not synonymous, thank God.

The good news is that while human beings worried about the continuation of their institution may present grim faces and sweaty palms, as missionary disciples we place our trust wholly in the God revealed in Jesus Christ who is very much in charge of past, present, and future through the Holy Spirit. In fact, as Craig Van Gelder reminds us, "Denominations are a fact of life in Christianity today, especially within the United States. But it is important to note that denominations as a form of the church of Jesus Christ in the world are of rather recent origins . . . . Denominations (are) less than 250 years old."[1] Not only is God's victory assured, but also with a careful eye to church history we see moments again and again where the church visible has waned only to be renewed by the Holy Spirit in God's good timing. Once again, rather than accomplishing this revival on his own, God has demonstrated a preferential option for seconding fragile, fallible human beings in the work of revival. One of my favorite examples is in the revival ministry offered by God through John Wesley. Wesley's witness still offers us important clues for how the Holy Spirit could be at work heating up our Laodicean lukewarm faith today.

John Wesley was born in England in 1703, the son of Samuel and Susanna Wesley. While his father was an Anglican priest it was his mother Susanna who had the most profound impact on John's spiritual development. Somewhat reluctantly, John studied for the priesthood at Oxford and entered "the family business" as a deacon in 1728. The next decade was a time of spiritual highs and lows as he attempted to "practice what he preached" and often came up wanting. In 1735 he left England for the new colony (now state) of Georgia in America. His missionary journey was a disaster and he fled with a broken heart and a pastoral reputation in tatters. John returned to England in a low state and reluctantly accepted an invitation from a friend to attend a small group study meeting at Aldersgate in London on May 24, 1738. While at the meeting something happened that changed Christ's church and God's mission in the world. John recorded in his diary:

> In the evening I went very unwillingly to a society in Aldersgate
> Street, where one was reading Luther's preface to the Epistle to the

1. Van Gelder, ed., *Missional Church,* 9. Van Gelder defines the older established or state churches as existing as the primary location of God's presence on earth through which the world can encounter God, with this authority being legitimated by the civil government. Denominational churches, however, exist as an organization with a purposive intent to accomplish something on behalf of God in the world, with this role being legitimated on a voluntary basis (18).

Romans. About a quarter before nine, while he was describing the change which God works in the heart through faith in Christ, I felt my heart strangely warmed. I felt I did trust in Christ, Christ alone, for salvation; and an assurance was given me that He had taken away my sins, even mine, and saved me from the law of sin and death.[2]

In response to this experience of God's pardoning love, John Wesley felt a renewed sense of mission and purpose in ministry. His enthusiasm, however, was not welcomed in many pulpits and soon he found himself with a dwindling number of places to preach. A friend from his Oxford days turned popular evangelist, George Whitefield, invited John and his brother Charles (also an Anglican priest) to join him in open-air preaching around Bristol in late March 1739.[3] While this method of proclamation was in direct conflict with Wesley's high church sensibilities, he accepted Whitefield's invitation and according to Charles they "broke down the bridge" and "became desperate" by embarking on the innovation using streets, fields, and gardens to preach God's Word.[4]

The response to Wesley's preaching was remarkable. For a large number of Britons who, due to the Industrial Revolution's migration from rural to urban areas, found themselves wholly without pastoral care due to an inflexible and outdated Church of England parish system, Wesley's proclamation of God's judgment and grace, love and assurance was a welcome and liberating message. Indeed, Wesley often avoided cathedral cities, deliberately seeking out the "underchurched industrial areas" ripe for evangelism.[5] It is interesting to compare the industrial revolution context of Wesley, with its solid Christendom base, to our current globalization, post-Christendom context for building mission communities in cultures of affluence in North America. In some ways, there is an advantage to our context that Wesley did not have as he encountered a powerful, well-financed institutional church that was highly resistant to reform. As Richard Bauckham notes:

> Can Christianity sufficiently detach itself from its own undoubted collusions with the oppressive metanarratives of western imperialism and progress to remain, between modern grand narrative and post-modern relativism, something else? One would think

2. Wesley, *The Journal of John Wesley*, May 24, 1738.

3. Rogal, "Counting the Congregation," 3.

4. Tyson, *Charles Wesley: A Reader*, 13.

5. Baker, "Real John Wesley," 192.

it should be easier for the church to distinguish itself from the forces of economic globalization than it used to be for the church to distinguish itself from western colonialism and cultural imperialism. After all, in the nineteenth and early twentieth centuries western culture really was more Christian than it is now, and so it was all too easy to confuse witness to Jesus with exporting western "Christian" culture. Now that western culture is increasingly post- and even anti-Christian, the distinction should be easier to make and to show.[6]

Perhaps it was his awareness of the powerful influence of the dominant eighteenth-century Christendom culture that made Wesley, unlike White-field, uncomfortable with simply having people hear the good news and then disperse. His upbringing of spiritual accountability, experience of leadership in the small groups at Oxford, and gifts of organization and ad-ministration convinced Wesley that open-air preaching must be followed up by the fellowship of a society.

Not long after his open-air preaching had begun there were many seeking after Wesley to know how to "flee from the wrath which is to come" and who asked him to "talk with us often, to direct and quicken us in our way, to give us the advices which you well know we need, and to pray with us, as well as for us."[7] Wesley agreed but soon realized there were far too many to visit individually and suggested instead, "If you will all of you come together every Thursday, in the evening, I will gladly spend some time with you in prayer, and give you the best advice I can."[8] Robert Moore argues that Wesley's choice was not an arbitrary one, rather, "Thursday night had been his turn at having the undivided attention of Susanna (his mother) in the Epworth parsonage. Susanna now provided him with his model for the exercise of pastoral authority as well as . . . his tactics of confronting it."[9] While Moore may exaggerate this connection of the specific day of the week, it is clear that Wesley's lifelong focus on his and others' spiritual growth prior to May 24, 1738 continued in the growth of his societies.

Despite the language of "fleeing from the wrath to come," the people called Methodist practiced a spirituality that included a deep engagement with the world—a pairing of evangelism and social justice. In this sense

6. Bauckham, *Bible and Mission*, 97.

7. Davies, ed., *Works of Wesley*, Volume 9, 256.

8. Ibid.

9. Moore, *Wesley and Authority*, 156–57.

Wesley's people were forerunners of what Roger Helland and Leonard Hjalmarson call "missional spirituality." Missional spirituality, according to Helland and Leonard,

> will avoid a common tendency to consign culture to the devil and huddle into the safety of Christian ghettos and subculture, replete with its own copied versions of music and movies, services and superstars, concerts and cruises. The cosmos and culture throb with God's will and work. All of life is sacred when we relate and submit all aspects of life to him. King David affirmed that God is everywhere and that we can't escape his presence. He asked, "Where can I go from your Spirit? Where can I flee from your presence?" (Psalm 139:7). It's in God that we "live and move and have our being" (Acts 17:28).[10]

In an industrialized, increasingly urban Britain, this missional spirituality was greatly needed, as the traditional catechesis of people moving from rural to urban parishes was increasingly ineffective. The Methodist societies became an entrepreneurial, ecclesiastical petri dish where people could receive catechesis and practice mentored discipleship in the local neighborhood. The purpose of these societies, which first emerged as a "company of men having the form, and seeking the power of godliness," was primarily one of instruction whereby the vital truths of the Christian faith were communicated, in particular to the poor and those who would never regularly enter an Anglican church.[11] Wesley's movement was growing not only in London but also throughout Britain, with "United Societies" forming in the wake of his evangelistic preaching. While at first the societies resembled many other Church of England-sponsored groups, as Wesley's preaching success grew so too did the membership that prompted a change in their structure. Wesley introduced the bands, which were cells of five to ten persons of the same sex and marital status, who "banded" together for spiritual nurture and support.[12]

These Wesleyan bands, according to Richard Heitzenrater, were "collegial groups that stressed nurture by means of mutual accountability, confession, and growth in grace through Christian fellowship and religious

---

10. Jelland and Hjalmarson, *Missional Spirituality,* 38.

11. Collins, *Real Christian,* 80.

12. Heitzenrater, *People Called Methodists,* 104.

conference."[13] Band members would ask each other at each meeting the following questions:

> What known sins have you committed since our last meetings?
> What temptations have you met with?
> How were you delivered?
> What have you thought, said or done, of which you doubt whether it be sin or not?[14]

The honest and deeply personal responses to these questions help foster an atmosphere of trust and mutual care that enabled members to bear each other's burdens and care for one another. As one of Charles Wesley hymns so aptly captured this goal:

> Help us to help each other, Lord
> Each other's cross to bear
> Let each his friendly aid afford,
> And feel his brother's care.
>
> Help us to build each other up,
> Our little stock improve;
> Increase our faith, confirm our hope,
> And perfect us in love.[15]

Over time, however, there were those whose spiritual maturity was greater than others and Wesley formed "select bands" for those who had received remission of sins and were leading an exemplary life.[16] But what should be done with the rest of the society members who were still struggling with their faith? Curiously, the solution to this spiritual problem came instead through a method devised to resolve a financial crisis.

The class meeting developed in early 1742 when a Methodist named Captain Foy suggested the beginning of a penny-a-week fund to help pay John Wesley's debt on a property in Bristol. Foy volunteered to collect from about twelve society members in his neighborhood and Wesley soon recognized the pastoral significance of this initiative. With Wesley's blessing the class meeting, consisting of up to twelve members, became a new subdivision of the larger Methodist society. The classes differed from the bands in many crucial ways: for instance, they were larger and were geographically

13. Ibid., 104–5.

14. Lim, "Wesleyan Preaching," 516.

15. Wakefield, *Methodist Spirituality*, 12.

16. Heitzenrater, *People Called Methodists*, 118.

orientated rather than divided by age, sex, or marital status. The classes included everyone in the society and not just those who "banded" together. This approach enabled the effective exercising of discipline among the whole society by leaders hand-picked by Wesley to discern whether "they were indeed working out their own salvation."[17] John Turner emphasized the importance of the class meetings by arguing they "became the means to ensure that there was genuine growth in discipleship, a means of evangelism and discipline that could be very rigorous," including the frequent expulsion of members who failed to continue to grow in grace.[18]

Removing members from the society was not done casually, however, and for those found slipping backwards in their spiritual progress in class meetings, Wesley developed something akin to a remedial classroom for Methodist dropouts. These groups became known as "penitential bands" and were comprised of "backslider members" who would be examined quarterly and either removed completely from the society or readmitted to the class meeting.[19] Emphasis on accountability for spiritual growth and fear of spiritual decline remained distinguishing marks that drew the ire of Wesley's Calvinist critics who endorsed predestination. As one scholar playfully observed, "A Methodist knows he's got religion but he's afraid he may lose it. A Presbyterian knows he can't lose it but he's afraid he hasn't got it."[20]

In 1743 Wesley published *The Nature and General Rules of the United Societies*, which indicated the normative value of the first two precepts of natural law (avoid evil; do good) as well as the importance of the means of grace such as praying, reading the Bible, and receiving the Lord's Supper.[21] These rules were offered not as the basis of justification, but as a guide, an illumination along the way, for those who were seeking the deeper graces of God.[22] Wesley's evangelical preaching, at best, awakened some to a justifying faith, but the rules he laid out for the United Societies ensured that those who gathered together might be systematically checked and encouraged to grow in God's sanctifying grace. The class meeting, then, became one of the principal vehicles for spiritual growth, accountability, and discipline by

17. Ibid., 119.

18. Turner, *John Wesley*, 47–48.

19. Heitzenrater, *People Called Methodists*, 124.

20. Turner, *John Wesley*, 32.

21. Collins, *Real Christian*, 81.

22. Ibid.

cross-referencing the behavior of those in attendance with the rules laid down by Wesley for the people called Methodist. For example, in 1743, Wesley removed several people from a society, from information obtained at a class meeting, because they disregarded the rules of the United Societies and were habitual in their Sabbath-breaking, drunkenness, spouse abuse, habitual lying, speaking evil, and the like. The class meeting, as Kenneth Collins concludes, enabled Wesley and other Methodist leaders to constantly prune the Methodist vine.[23]

Of course, societies within the Church of England were common. So what made the United Societies unique and so popular? John Kent has convincingly argued that Wesley's societies were the only places where the "primary religion" impulses of certain social groups, especially within the Church of England, could be satisfied.[24] Primary religion, quite separate from elaborate theological frameworks developed by "religious professionals," is the human impulse to seek the connection with an intrusive supernatural power that can both aid one's successes and limit difficulties from other humans or spiritual forces.[25] Wesley's ability to read his British context was similar to Lesslie Newbigin's over two hundred years later, understanding that "God accepts human culture . . . and God judges human culture."[26] This acceptance and judgment of God includes "church culture." As the Parish Collective cautions:

> Without a dynamic living tradition shaped by the Spirit in a particular place, this once tangible expression of the church can because these traditions can be calcified into a set of denominational beliefs and liturgical practices disconnected from everyday realities. Professor Michael Warren goes so far as to say that "liturgy as aesthetics is a sham if not bonded to the loveliness of a life of struggle for fidelity."[27]

By the early eighteenth century there was a large gap between what ordinary people needed from the gospel and what the established church offered. Thus, Wesleyan Methodism reached a wide constituency by responding to the unfulfilled primary religious demands of many Britons defined as a "passionate hunger for access to invisible powers that promised to change

23. Collins, *Real Christian*, 81.

24. Kent, *Wesley and the Wesleyans*, 1.

25. Ibid., 6–7.

26. Newbigin, *Gospel in a Pluralistic Culture*, 195.

27. Sparks, Soerens, and Friesen, eds., *New Parish*, 79.

the life and prosperity of the adherent."[28] It is fascinating to note how the Holy Spirit's revival under Wesley has similar marks to those of the Missional Church identified by Craig Van Gelder and Rick Rouse in God's movement of his people:

FROM:	TO:
Maintenance	Mission
Membership	Discipleship
Pastor-Centered	Lay-Empowered
Chaplaincy (self)	Hospitality (others)
Focus on ourselves	Focus on the World
Settled	Sent[29]

Methodist societies distinguished themselves from their Church of England small group contemporaries by their emphasis on the belief that in their midst was a real and present "supernatural force" that offered personal protection, cure for diseases, ecstatic experience, and prophetic guidance.[30] With this growth in church structure came a warning from Wesley, however, lest Methodists should become preoccupied with governance and lose touch with primary religion. Wesley cautioned, "I am not afraid that the people called Methodists should ever cease to exist either in Europe or America. But I am afraid, lest they should only exist as a dead sect, having the form of religion without the power."[31]

Once again, it is important to note that while Wesley's skill for organizing followers into "connexion" is clear, the mature societies of the late 1740s were a product of serendipitous and experimental ecclesiology

28. Ibid., 8.

29. Rouse and Van Gelder, *Field Guide*, 23.

30. Wesley also began to recognize that many of those around him were gifted preachers. Wesley soon created "rounds," later called circuits, and authorized those who demonstrated preaching abilities in their local societies to be full-time paid traveling preachers known as "itinerants." They were given spiritual charge of a round and worked through their jurisdiction systematically over a period of four to six weeks. Every two years or less Wesley moved them onto another circuit. The itinerants, like all the societies, were in "connexion" with Wesley as well as with each other. This "connexion" proved to be a vital foundation to future Methodist discipline and government. For more information see Geoffrey Milburn and Margaret Batty, eds., *Workaday Preachers: The Story of Methodist Local Preaching*. Wesley further developed this close-knit family-like structure to include an annual conference that met for a few days at Wesley's invitation. The Conference, according to Frank Baker, served as a consultative body whose function was to help Wesley arrive at decisions in his administration of the Methodist societies.

31. Carter Jr., "Recovering Human Nature," 53.

and that Wesley developed his model from "trial and error, borrowing and adaptation, occasionally outright invention."[32] A fundamental principle of Wesley's understanding of church, according to Henry Rack, was that "order in the church should be simply what is expedient and necessary for sustaining the preaching of the gospel and fostering its fruits."[33] Suggestions from other clergy and members of the United Societies, as well as Wesley's prior experience in both Anglican and Moravian small group ministry, all combined to fashion the unique elements of the Methodist societies.

The evolving structure of Methodism following Wesley's assurance of faith on May 24, 1738 ensured that members of the United Societies would remain accountable for spiritual growth to God and one another. Wesley developed an ecclesiastical structure (within the larger framework of the Church of England) that was both flexible and responsive to the needs of evangelical mission. Wesley's administrative gifts and his willingness to borrow ideas from others created an effective community of accountability known as the United Societies. As Robert Moore argues, "Effective as his preaching was, the success of his movement was insured by his development of a means of continued contact and control of those who responded to him. It was one thing to respond in a positive manner to his preaching—it was quite another to try to sustain the alteration in lifestyle which was assumed to be the result of such a response."[34] Indeed, Wesley and his itinerants awakened many to a justifying faith through preaching, but the real key to the Methodist movement was the gathering of these awakened individuals in communities of accountable discipleship where they continued to experience sanctifying faith.

While Wesley's methods for organization were fluid and at times *ad hoc*, not unlike John Calvin's pragmatic gospel imagination, Wesley argued that his ultimate purpose for organization always remained focused on nothing less than the "pursuit of inward and outward holiness in the last analysis the hope of perfection."[35] Wesley's famous phrase, "the whole world is my parish," was as much a rebuke of failed ecclesiology as a grandiose vision of the Methodist movement. Wesley's missional spirituality understood that missiology shapes ecclesiology "as the Father sent the Son, energized by the Spirit, so the Son sends the church, also energized

32. Rack, *Reasonable Enthusiast*, 237.

33. Ibid.

34. Moore, *John Wesley and Authority*, 152.

35. Rack, *Reasonable Enthusiast*, 249.

by the Spirit," equipping people to be "incarnational missionaries in their communities and workplaces who know how to exegete and engage culture and live the gospel in deed and world."[36] Wesley's societies differed from other Anglican societies in that they offered members unapologetic access to "primary religion" experiences that were frowned upon in most other communities of England's established church.

This is an important note for missional leaders in a culture of North American affluence. As Soong-Chan Rah notes in his critique of the Church's western cultural captivity,

> The acquiescence to consumer culture means that churches fall into the vicious cycle of trying to keep the attendees happy. When a church entices consumers by using marketing techniques and materialistic considerations, is it possible to change that approach after the individual begins attending the church? Or has it set up the church in such a way that the church attendee expects the same level of accommodation that was available when they were church shopping? Can a relationship that began on the level of an exchange of goods and services transition to a deeper level of commitment? Even when the church seeks to develop a small group ministry that would deepen the member's involvement, the establishing of that small group community falls along certain lines of affinity, so that now the church consumerism is shopping for a small group that meets his or her criteria or personal preferences. Breaking through a consumer mindset that is dominant in the culture and has found its way into the church becomes more and more difficult. Materialism and consumerism become the enticement into the church but also the trap of maintaining and growing the church.[37]

John Wesley developed a countercultural system of mutual accountability that resisted personal preference and preserving social status when forming small group ministries. Wesley's organizational skills and focus on accountability and spiritual growth are, according to A. Raymond George, why John, rather than Charles or George Whitefield, became the "acknowledged leader of the Methodists and in some sense the founder of a new branch of the Christian church."[38] Indeed, near the end of his life, George Whitefield affirmed Wesley's gift of developing a superior evangelical structure when

36. Jelland and Hjalmarson, *Missional Spirituality*, 216.

37. Rah, *Next Evangelicalism*, 55.

38. Stacey, ed., *John Wesley*, 108.

he said, "My brother Wesley acted wisely. The souls that were awakened under his ministry he joined in class, and thus preserved the fruits of his labor. This I neglected, and my people are a rope of sand."[39]

Whenever studying "heroes" in church history there is often the temptation to lift them out of their historical context as solutions to contemporary ecclesiastical challenges. John Wesley is an easy mark for this limiting approach as he stands for many as a symbol of successful evangelism and mission whose solutions to church decline and the breakdown of moral order could be a quick fix for today's post-Christendom reality in North America. In response to this temptation John Turner warns against those "who may be tempted still to imagine him as an eighteenth-century Billy Graham, but always on a horse or a market cross" and insists that Wesley must be understood within his own particular and peculiar context.[40] To view Wesley as the forerunner of contemporary television evangelists most importantly betrays his absolute conviction that the United Societies were to be both communities of worship and action, places that enabled people to proclaim God's Word and be practitioners of God's love. Aubin de Gruchy reminds us that Wesley's ministry must be seen through a lens of both evangelism and social service as he concludes, "Clearly, for Wesley, there could be no distancing of the 'personal' gospel from the 'social' gospel. They went hand in hand. There was only the one Gospel expressed both personally and socially."[41]

Despite the ever-present danger of misinterpretation, John Wesley's life and legacy can continue to be a source of strength and inspiration for Christ's church in the world. For Christians, Wesley offers great potential for insight and formation if one is willing to walk the tightrope between history and hagiography, inspiration and idolatry. As Howard Slaatte argues, "Much of what Wesley emphasized is still needed in the contemporary church if it is to be as positive in its message and as influential in its outreach to this generation, as Wesley would expect it to be."[42]

This gift from Wesley to Christians today is the emphasis on the value of the covenanted community as a place of accountability for spiritual growth in one's discipleship. Wesley's Holy Spirit-driven, missional

---

39. Collins, *Real Christian*, 81.

40. Turner, *John Wesley*, vii.

41. de Gruchy, "Beyond Intention," 77.

42. Slaatte, *Wesley's Theology*, v.

approach to Christian community recognized the "balancing couplet" that Craig Van Gelder has identified as follows:

> The church is always forming (missional)—*ecclesia semper formanda.* The church is always reforming (confessional)—*ecclesia semper reformanda.*

By this, Van Gelder means that missional leaders and communities are always forming in relation to new contexts where they seek to be relevant while, on the other hand, they are always reforming in relation to the historical witness of the Christian tradition.[43] Wesley went to great lengths to be clear that while the Holy Spirit was doing a new thing in their local context, it was part of the Holy Spirit's continuing witness rooted within the Church of England and broader catholic witness of the gospel.

While scholars continue to debate the purpose and mission of the church today, it has been suggested that the Christian church should primarily be a community of prayer and compassion.[44] To this, Wesley would add that mission communities of faith are also places of accountability for spiritual growth. While Wesley's preaching (and that of his itinerants) awakened many to a justifying faith, the strength of the Methodist movement lay in its ability to gather people together in communities of accountable discipleship to experience sanctifying grace. Today, this strength of mutual spiritual examination and confession continues to empower people for God's work in the world and sustains individuals as they move through their own pilgrimage of faith. Indeed, Wesley's experience and leadership made certain that the strength of the United Societies included accountability of members to God and one another that provided fertile ground for a sustained growth in holiness through discipleship.

Wesleyan small group ministry was not about asking, "What color should we paint the fellowship hall?" but "What known sins have you committed since our last meeting?" or "Have you nothing you desire to keep secret?"[45] This is not to suggest, of course, that practical matters like physical property maintenance are irrelevant; rather that Wesley himself believed that he had discovered "the key of mutual accountability in fellowship as the critical and distinguishing mark of the movement."[46] These

43. Van Gelder, *Ministry of the Missional Church,* 54.

44. Borg, *Meeting God Again,* 122–27.

45. Davies, ed., *Works of Wesley,* Volume 9, 78.

46. Chilcote, *Wesleyan Tradition,* 32.

close-knit communities of prayer, compassion, and accountability enabled strangers to become friends and together they were transformed by God's grace as they shared their "pilgrimages of faith."[47]

Certainly many Christian communities include the gift of small group ministry in their formation of disciples today. Missional leadership in a culture of affluence pays particular attention to the small group's impact on the local neighborhood—including where I live in the Pacific Northwest. With its sea of bright, shiny glass condo towers full of young profession-als, downtown Vancouver presents an exciting opportunity and challenge for church planting in one of the most "secular" parts of North America. I mentioned the church plant called St. Peter's Fireside earlier. A student at our college is currently serving as the Pastor of Discipleship for this new mission community in downtown Vancouver. Roger told me that lately the church plant has been connecting with an "older crowd" than they expect-ed. "Really?" I said, "How old?" "Oh, they are mostly in their late twenties." "That's a problem most churches would love to have," I told him. Roger has developed a small group ministry across the downtown most nights of the week in people's condos. What I found most encouraging is the method he is using for the small group meeting:

Week One: Upward—a focus on Bible study and conversations about the nature of God revealed in Jesus Christ.

Week Two: Inward—a reflection on the state of their discipleship and desire to grow in holiness. A time to pray with, and for, one another.

Week Three: Outward—a commitment to be in the neighborhood as a small group and work in a ministry or social ser-vice institution that is involved in acts of justice and mercy.

One of the many ways that the Holy Spirit uses small group ministries as a "missional microwave" is as an incubator for God's love and grace that em-power people for their own public ministry. This key step of empowerment, cautiously endorsed and at times even contained by Wesley, proved to be a key growth strategy for the Methodist revival movement. These mission communities, founded in the wake of evangelical preaching and sustained by accountable discipleship, in turn birthed evangelists of their own. This established a pattern of growth that required both the justifying impact

47. Ibid., 32.

of the itinerant preachers and the sanctifying power of the United Societies. In addition, as the Methodist movement grew throughout the 1740s, it stressed a balance in its work and witness between evangelism and social service. This care of the soul and the needs of society became a hallmark of Methodism in Wesley's day and beyond.

Wesley's warning to us, in light of John Kent's recent scholarship, is that if we abandon the work of evangelism we run the risk of losing touch with the primary religion impulse of people to feel and experience the God of grace and glory.[48] Kent reminds us that humans yearn to experience the divine on a primary level yet many religious institutions remain primarily on the level of secondary theologies, interpreting and ordering others' experiences. In missional leadership language Allan Roxburgh refers to this as a legitimacy challenge for denominations. Roxburgh explains legitimacy by arguing:

> We make sense of our particular moment in time by placing interpretive frameworks around periods and events; we create meaning from a storehouse of narratives, metaphors, and myths. The narrative frameworks that shape a culture at a particular time exist because people find in them the resources to shape their lives in relationship to the surrounding context. The legitimacy of a narrative involves its ability to provide an explanatory framework that addresses a group's back understanding of life and that provides them with a means of successfully ordering that life. Organizations such as governments or denominations lose legitimacy when they cease to hold sufficient loyalty, commitment or authority from people. This loss has been happening across denominational systems: they are confronting a legitimacy crisis and will be unable to become missionally shaped systems unless they understand the dynamics of this crisis.[49]

By the eighteenth century the Church of England had a legitimacy crisis. Its secondary theological interpretations of the world were so elaborate and intellectualized that they were noticeably removed and set apart from the primary religion impulse of the people. Responding to this need, John Wesley, through his Methodist societies, both awakened and sustained

48. Kent, *Wesley and the Wesleyans*, 8. Kent argues that what got Wesleyan Methodism off the ground in the 1740s was the Wesleys' encounter with and response to the demands of primary religion, a passionate hunger for access to invisible powers, and so for ways to change the life and prosperity of the adherent.

49. Van Gelder, ed., *Missional Church and Denominations*, 81.

this primary religious impulse in a way that the Church of England's parish system was ill equipped to even attempt. Wesley's societies provided a sustaining and sanctifying community where God's transforming presence was palpable and discipleship practically applied, in direct contrast to the structured, predictable, and lifeless Church of England in the eighteenth century. It is possible to hypothesize that today's growth of evangelical and Pentecostal churches is due, in part, to their ability to respond to and shape community life and practice in ways that address the needs of people to experience this primary religious impulse. David Martin supports this argument in his work on the growth of global Pentecostalism where he defines the strength of the eighteenth-century Methodist movement as "finding the supernatural in the fabric of everyday life."[50] Describing early Methodism as "the first wave of competitive religious entrepreneurship," Martin argues that on a global scale Pentecostalism surpassed Methodism by replicating the eighteenth-century Wesleyan spirit "in its entrepreneurship and adaptability, lay participation and enthusiasm, and in its splintering and fractiousness."[51]

We are called to mission that both sanctifies believers on the inside and reaches outwards at the same time with a justifying proclamation of evangelism and social service that addresses the primary religious needs of others and unites them for God's work in the world. Today we find ourselves in a world at least as troubled and restless as in the times of our Methodist ancestors in the Christian faith, and yet with hope we continue forward in mission drawing our strength from the Word of God and our purpose from the words of John Wesley, who said,

> God loves you: therefore love and obey him. Christ dies for you: therefore die to sin. Christ is risen: therefore rise in the image of God. Christ liveth evermore: therefore live to God, till you live with him in glory. So we preached; and so you believed. This is the scriptural way, the Methodist way, the true way.[52]

50. Martin, *Pentecostalism*, 7.

51. Ibid., 8.

52. Quoted in Outler, ed., *John Wesley*, 237.

Chapter Ten

Hurry on Down—the Price is Right
(Zacchaeus-Like Faith in the World Today)

God put fingers on our hand for money to slide through them so He can give us
more. Whatever a person gives away, God will reimburse.

—Martin Luther

A whole generation of us in North America was raised on the dazzling
array of consumer choices offered by Bob Barker daily on *The Price
is Right*. Who could resist the capitalism-driven game show that challenged competitors to guess the correct price of products and work their
way through an epic quest of games towards the "showcase showdown"?
This narrative of "Purchaser's Progress" was narrated by the one and only
three-piece suited, fine-quaffed–hair-sporting Bob Barker, with his long
skinny microphone and signature line, "Come on down." The mildly ec-
centric game show host once said, "Nothing gives me quite so much joy
as when people tell me they've had their pets spayed or neutered." Hmm,
curious. Bob also said, "You can't fool television viewers with dancing girls
and flashing lights." Funny, it seemed to have worked on most of us kids
growing up. But the line I appreciate the most from Bob Barker was, "I'll tell

you one thing, in what I do for a living, there's no substitute for experience. I don't care how much natural talent you may have . . . . In the type of show I do, you can depend on surprises."

I love that. For the man who spent a lifetime inviting others to "come on down" came to rely on surprises. When we summarize the movement from Botox to bypass, from a Laodicean lukewarm faith to a vibrant, missionally focused impact on our neighborhood, we need to live with an expectation of revelation. As missionary disciples, we need to listen to the One whose voice is invitational and whose call to "come and follow me" is full of surprises.

One of the most delightful missional moments in the New Testament has to be the story of Zacchaeus. Now we don't know a lot about Zacchaeus but the Bible does give us some crucial information. Zacchaeus was a chief tax collector and he was rich. He was also a wee little man who may or may not have suffered from small man syndrome. Here's how Luke records the encounter:

> Jesus entered Jericho and was passing through. A man was there
> by the name of Zacchaeus; he was a chief tax collector and was
> wealthy. He wanted to see who Jesus was, but because he was short
> he could not see over the crowd. So he ran ahead and climbed a
> sycamore-fig tree to see him, since Jesus was coming that way.[1]

Why should we care about his profession or the fact that he was wealthy? First of all, it is important to know about how tax collectors, and chief tax collectors at that, were employed in the Roman Empire. We touched on this briefly while exploring the parable of the Pharisee and Tax Collector in the temple. To remind you, this is not a simple comparison to Revenue Canada or the Internal Revenue Service. In a church I served there were a good number of local Revenue Canada employees in the pews and they loved tax collector stories. One tax collector once asked me the difference between a taxidermist and a tax collector shaking hands on a Sunday at the door. He informed me without even waiting for an answer that *the taxidermist only takes the skin*. Ugh. While tax collecting today may be unpopular it was even more problematic in Jesus' day for different reasons. The Romans were big into census events or carefully recording the population of the various provinces of the empire. Jesus himself was born during one of these moments that required Mary and Joseph and the donkey to

1. Luke 19:1–4, *NIV*.

travel to Bethlehem. Census was so important to the Romans because of tax revenue. Here's how it worked: based on the population of a certain region confirmed by census, they would tender the tax collecting service out to a local entrepreneur, making clear that given the number of people in this region the Romans expected X number of dollars/denarii for that area. The entrepreneur, called the chief tax collector, would put the money out front to the Roman government. The Romans were happy because they had their money without an elaborate bureaucracy, let alone having to go door to door in a conquered territory. That unenviable task fell to the chief tax collector. Well, he wasn't about to start knocking on doors, so he hired locals to be his tax collectors. In Jesus' day these people were despised since they were tasked with not only getting enough money from the local people to cover the amount for Rome, but they were also lining their own pockets, as well as keeping the chief tax collector in the lifestyle he had grown accustomed to! The chief tax collector was the worst kind of person—he was a thief. He was working for the occupying army and he claimed to be a faithful Jew. Now we get a sense of why Zacchaeus was so despised by the local people.

Despite Zacchaeus's poor reputation amongst the locals, he appears curious and has heard a lot about this famous rabbi named Jesus. As word travels through Jericho that Jesus is coming, people line the streets to have a look. Zacchaeus is swept up in the excitement and does two things that are odd given the social codes of that day. First, he runs. It was considered undignified for a grown man to run in public, a little like the father running to greet the prodigal son on his return to the farm. Second, Zacchaeus climbs a tree. Climbing trees was a silly, childish, absurd action not done by men of importance like the chief tax collector. Added to this is the delightful irony that the sycamore tree produced an inferior type of fig that was consumed by the poor. This is like Donald Trump standing on top of a food bank donation box straining to see President Obama's motorcade wind through the streets of New York on the way to the United Nations. It just doesn't happen. But there Zaccchaeus was as a bystander to the day's events, bouncing on a sycamore tree branch, visible to the disapproving townsfolk. The sight made children snicker and point in amusement. But the greatest shock was still to come.

I imagine Jesus and his disciples before this story busy all day going about the kind of dignitary duties you might expect important people to perform on a visit to a new place. Perhaps we could imagine Jesus giving a couple of interviews to the *Jericho Journal* newspaper, cutting a ribbon at the newly remodeled Joshua fought the Battle of Jericho and the walls came tumbling town museum, gift shop, and cafeteria. I see him strolling through town with all the important people and receiving dinner invitations from all kinds of influential folks from the mayor to the president of the Chamber of Commerce. But the Holy Spirit had a different plan. As Jesus walks through the streets the people are cheering and waving, Jesus acknowledges them with his warm smile and compassionate presence. Jesus' eyes, however, are fixed on something—no—someone else. Seeing an odd wee man in a sycamore tree surrounded only by children in nearby trees Jesus leans over to the mayor and says, "Who is that up there?" "That," the mayor spits in response, "is Zacchaeus, the chief tax collector. Don't bother with him." Jesus turns to the person on the other side and asks, "What do you know about that man?" "Zacchaeus," snorts the man beside him, "he's a cheat and a thief—don't worry, one day when we kick the Romans out we'll deal with him." "That man," pipes up another person walking with them, "is a sinner, he is totally beyond salvation." And with that, Jesus stops suddenly beneath the tree. The crowd is startled at first and then slightly amused to see Jesus talking to this character in the tree. Tearing up the posh dinner invitations in his hands, Jesus shouts, "Hurry on down Zacchaeus, for tonight I am going to dine at your house." The crowd is first puzzled and then angry as they see Jesus going to the home of the chief tax collector.

Imagine this next scene as Jesus and his disciples sit with Zacchaeus and some of his tax collecting friends having dinner. If you think it's odd and perhaps even a little rude for our Savior to invite himself over for dinner, again the social code of the day is at work. Zacchaeus's house was seen as ritually impure by those religious folks since tax collectors entered various homes and inspected goods. By entering Zacchaeus's, home Jesus, whose reputation was as a holy man, would overcome that stigma, thus doing Zacchaeus a big favor. Imagine Jesus laughing and sharing a meal with Zacchaeus, teaching him about the kingdom of God and the requirements of discipleship, forgiving past wrongs and offering this crooked and lonely tax collector love and friendship—perhaps for the first time. Imagine the flicker of candlelight, the clinking of wine glasses, and the darting eyes of townspeople through the windows, eavesdropping on everything taking place.

What I find fascinating is that Jesus didn't wait in a synagogue or church for Zacchaeus to show up and confess his sin. No, in a missional move, Jesus and his disciples encountered Zacchaeus out in the community and invited *themselves* over for dinner. Funny, we are commissioned as missionary disciples to "go and tell" yet so often we reduce God's sending of the church into the world to "come and hear." Jesus and his disciples lived with an expectation that this neighbor had something he could offer *them*. God is always on the move towards us, seeking a loving relationship. The Bible records what happens in this grace-filled table fellowship moment:

> When Jesus got to the tree, he looked up and said, "Zacchaeus, hurry down. Today is my day to be a guest in your home." Zacchaeus scrambled out of the tree, hardly believing his good luck, delighted to take Jesus home with him. Everyone who saw the incident was indignant and grumped, "What business does he have getting cozy with this crook?" Zacchaeus just stood there, a little stunned. He stammered apologetically, "Master, I give away half my income to the poor—and if I'm caught cheating, I pay four times the damages." Jesus said, "Today is salvation day in this home! Here he is: Zacchaeus, son of Abraham! For the Son of Man came to find and restore the lost."[2]

A colleague of mine at the Vancouver School of Theology, Rabbi Laura Duhan-Kaplan, helped me understand what was taking place in this story from a Jewish perspective. Laura told me once that rabbis have historically prescribed a delightful fourfold method for forgiveness that brings lasting change and reconciliation. The four steps are:

Know you have done something wrong.
Feel really bad about it.
Attempt to make amends.
Don't do it again.

I love that. The approach is simple without being simplistic. Zacchaeus is aware he has wronged others. His remorse is genuine and strong. He promises to make amends: "Look, Lord! Here and now I give half of my possessions to the poor, and if I have cheated anybody out of anything, I will pay back four times the amount."[3] And, like most biblical characters, once they have served their purpose they fade to the background and we're not sure what happens next in their lives. I think it is safe to say, however, that after his encounter with Jesus Zacchaeus lived with a strong desire not to do wrong to others again.

2. Luke 19:5–10, *The Message.*
3. Luke 19:8, *NIV.*

Zacchaeus, a man with a shady past, showed up that day to be a bystander, but through the experience of Jesus' grace-filled presence and his forgiving love, Zacchaeus becomes an active player on God's kingdom team. This missional experience of moving from bystander to participant in the kingdom of God transformed Zacchaeus's life. It was not just his encounter with Jesus, but the opportunity to reflect on that experience and his whole life experience that led to the transformation. In a sense, Zacchaeus's story highlights philosopher Immanuel Kant's teaching that all human experience is *interpreted experience* since it is *mediated* through our pre-existing intellectual concepts. To say it differently, while we are always moving forward down the road of life, we are making sense of our direction based on a regular glance at the rearview mirror. Indeed, the church's history is full of people who, through the Spirit of God, have looked in the rearview mirror and reflected upon that experience were transformed. It took St. Augustine many years through various philosophical groups and religious expressions to finally become a Christian bearing witness to his line, "our hearts are restless, O God, until they find their rest in you." It took John Wesley ten years after ordination before God helped him finally made sense of his life experience and he could write, "I felt my heart strangely warmed." It took John Newton countless years as a slave ship captain before he realized that his lifestyle was full of sin and God changed his ways, helping him to scribble out the famous words, "Amazing grace, how sweet the sound that saved a wretch like me."

How about us? Do we pretend like this kind of life-changing experience is only limited to the past, to biblical characters like Zacchaeus or historical characters like Wesley? Absolutely not. Living and loving as a missionary disciple in the world reminds us that God is still at work in our lives today. Sometimes, it is only when we stop to look in that rearview mirror that it is possible, by grace, to make sense of it all.

I remember years ago asking a quiet, dignified man in my church if he would like to offer a brief testimony in the upcoming Sunday service. Surprisingly, this man who did not sit on any committee nor appear in any leadership roles said yes. At faith sharing time, he made his way up to the pulpit and shared a story of when he was with the Canadian Army during the Second World War. Out for a Sunday morning skate on Labrador Bay, he relished the crisp winter air and was quite a sight flowing across the ice in his green army kit. Suddenly, without warning, the ice gave way and he plunged into the frigid water. With skates and heavy kit on, he quickly sank into the murky darkness of the water. He looked up frantically at the disappearing light of the little hole in the ice above. He knew he was going to die and all he could think of was the telegram his mother would receive and her broken heart. He prayed to God and suddenly, he received a shot of energy unlike he could ever ask for or imagine. Kicking off his heavy kit he made his way to the surface. Grabbing onto the ice, the first piece broke off in his hands. He tried again and again until finally he crawled up on the surface. Half frozen, he made way to the aid station and lived. As the image of the young and lean, half-frozen soldier faded from our minds, all that was left was a gentle, grey-haired man leaning on the pulpit without a whisper to be heard in the sanctuary. His concluding words were spoken in a hush, like a benediction. "You know," he said with a quiet confidence, "from that day forward, I learned to trust Jesus and I've never looked back."

The joy of offering missional leadership in a culture of affluence is the front row seat we get to witness the Holy Spirit turning people away from crass materialism and empty values, towards a relationship with the living God we know in Jesus Christ. There is a price, of course, but it is worth it.

Years ago a husband and wife joined in regular worship at our congregation. Neither of them were Christians, but through some Christian friends and the hospitality of the local church, they started worshipping week by week. They asked a million questions, attended our Christianity 101 course, and started to engage in the disciplines of following Jesus. After a year they asked if they could be baptized in Sunday worship. I was thrilled, as were the elders of the church. A few days before the baptism Sunday they came to meet with me in the church office. We engaged in a little small talk but I sensed they had come to ask a specific question. Eventually they got around to their real purpose of the visit. "My wife and I were just wondering, um, how much does it cost to be baptized?" I was caught off guard and taken a little aback. I stammered, "Oh it doesn't cost anything, it's God's grace, it's free." They seemed pleased and after a few more minutes of chat they left to continue their day.

As soon as they left my office, I knew that I had made a mistake. I wanted to call after them but they were already out of the building. I sat back down at my desk and looked at the text for Sunday's service:

> When Jesus saw the crowd around him, he gave orders to cross to the other side of the lake. Then a teacher of the law came to him and said, "Teacher, I will follow you wherever you go." Jesus replied, "Foxes have dens and birds have nests, but the Son of Man

has no place to lay his head." Another disciple said to him, "Lord, first let me go and bury my father." But Jesus told him, "Follow me, and let the dead bury their own dead."[4]

That Sunday as we celebrated the baptism of these two adult converts to Christianity, people who were engaged by missionary disciples in the community, welcomed to "belong before they believed" within the worshipping life of the church, and who encountered the risen Christ through his broken yet beloved body, I spoke about the cost of discipleship. I apologized for giving the answer that "it costs nothing to follow Jesus." I was wrong. I told the congregation that, in fact, it costs *everything*—our whole lives. By turning our whole lives over to Christ, however, we participate in the joy and victory of the Son of God in this world—a victory achieved long before we were ever asked to give our "yes" to God's grace-filled invitation to discipleship. It's a little like Karl Barth's famous answer to when he was saved, "I was saved 2,000 years ago on a hill outside Jerusalem named Calvary." In the end, following Jesus costs everything since it cost the Son of God his life. It's a high price. But the price is right.

4. Matthew 8:18–22, *NIV.*

Conclusion

Silver and Gold I Have None
—The Laodicean Cure?

The last part of a man to be converted is his wallet.

—John Wesley

Growing up on the Canadian prairies, winters came early and stayed late. In fact, I'm not sure I remember a Halloween where there wasn't at least a little bit of snow on the ground. I know some Christians are against celebrating Halloween, but in my house there was always a distinction between not celebrating anSything demonic and gladly participating in a candy grab from neighbors.[1] As a child every year I'd work so hard on

---

1. The origins of Halloween are undoubtedly pagan. Its earliest roots are found in Samhain (pronounced *sow-in*), the Celtic harvest festival at the end of October that marked the beginning of winter and a bridge to the world of the dead through the transition of seasons. The Romans conquered parts of the Celtic region in the first century AD and added their own celebrations to the mix, including Feralia, another day set aside to honor the dead, and the festival of Pomona, named for the goddess of fruit and trees. When Christianity hooked up with Constantinian power in the fourth century AD, church leaders started to eliminate the pagan influence in the empire. On November 1, 731 AD, Pope Gregory III consecrated a chapel in St. Peter's Basilica in Rome to all

my costume and never, ever got to wear it outside. You see in Winnipeg it would snow and be so cold that you'd have to put your full snowsuit on, that made you feel like a NASA astronaut, and then you'd put on the itchy, multicolored, hand-knit toque from Grandma's house—you know, Grandma's house where fashion goes to die—or at least that's what I thought as a kid. And then, just when it couldn't get any worse your mum would come at you like a snake handler with the long double-length scarf that she would wrap around your head so fast that you looked like an extra from the movie *Lawrence of Arabia*. Then, and only then, could you add some sort of token pirate hat or clown mask to go out trick-or-treating.

Out you'd go down the street, in our little 1950s suburban development, the white pillowcase bouncing on the frozen sidewalk up and down snow-covered driveways—your mum or dad standing at the sidewalk waiting, shifting their weight uneasily from one foot to the other. You'd knock on the door and have to say "Halloween apples!" or "Trick or treat!" or, if you thought it was an especially promising-looking house that would give good candy, you might give them the full "Trick or treat, smell my feet, give me something good to eat, not too big, not too small, just the size of Montreal."

And it worked perfectly every year. Well, except for the one house on our street. You know that house—neatly kept yard, nicely shoveled walk, nondescript bungalow with the older couple living in it, the porch light always on, so you'd run up expecting the pillowcase to gain more treasure. You'd shout "trick or treat" but when the elderly couple answered the door they did not have the usual bowl in their hands full of candy, no, they had a pile of leaflets. No candy was coming. Instead it was a tract emblazoned with the name JESUS on it. You'd watch the brochure float down into the bag, like the last leaf of autumn falling from a frozen tree, you'd look down in the bag, you'd look up, you'd look down again, and close the bag and walk away. *Tricked, not treated.* At the end of the driveway my good Baptist mother would be standing there smiling. "What's up with those people Mum?" I

Christian martyrs and ordered an annual observance in the city. By the ninth century, the first day of November was celebrated throughout the church as "All Saints" or "All Hallows," with the day before known as "All Hallows' Eve," shortened over time to "Halloween." I wouldn't advocate "celebrating" Halloween but I am not against participating in trick-or-treating as I'm personally less worried about the devil showing up on my doorstep and asking for candy on All Hallows' Eve and more worried about letting the tempter sneak into my life the rest of the year by denying Christ in my words and actions in everyday discipleship.

would say in disgust. And every year my mother would offer the same line: "Well dear, they love God too, they just love him a little bit *differently*."

Would you believe that was the same way that people in the temple long ago would have looked at the apostles in the early days of the church: "Those people love God too, they just love God a little differently"? Peter and John were faithful Jews after all, *talmadim* or disciples of an upstart rabbi from Galilee, executed by the Romans for sedition against the state. Followers of this rabbi named Yeshua were now spreading like wildfire in the city with an amazing witness that what humanity had killed God had raised to new life.

Peter and John were, of course, two of the major leaders of this movement, synagogue school dropouts who had taken up the family business of fishing and were called by Jesus to "Come and follow me," to be about the business of fishing for people. If Peter and John were Canadian, they'd wear hockey jerseys with a big C (captain) and an A (assistant captain) in the corner to show they were on Jesus' team and important leaders.

In the book of Acts Luke records a missional encounter Peter and John have in the neighborhood:

> One day Peter and John were going up to the temple at the time of prayer—at three in the afternoon. Now a man who was lame from birth was being carried to the temple gate called Beautiful, where he was put every day to beg from those going into the temple courts. When he saw Peter and John about to enter, he asked them for money. Peter looked straight at him, as did John. Then Peter said, "Look at us!" So the man gave them his attention, expecting to get something from them. Then Peter said, "Silver or gold I do not have, but what I do have I give you. In the name of Jesus Christ of Nazareth, walk." Taking him by the right hand, he helped him up, and instantly the man's feet and ankles became strong. He jumped to his feet and began to walk. Then he went with them into the temple courts, walking and jumping, and praising God. When all the people saw him walking and praising God, they recognized him as the same man who used to sit begging at the temple gate called Beautiful, and they were filled with wonder and amazement at what had happened to him.[2]

Peter and John, good pious Jews, were heading up to the temple for "evening prayers"—a little misleading since it was late afternoon. As they approach the beautiful gate they met a crippled man begging. The crippled man was

2. Acts 3:1–10, *NIV*.

sat at the beautiful gate, day after day, full of expectation. He expected silver and gold to fall into his lap like children on Halloween evening expect sweet treats to fall into their pillowcases. The crippled man never counted on two pious Jews named Peter and John to offer anything else. In fact, like a homeless beggar in a large North American city, the Bible suggest that this man didn't even look up at the swirling crowds moving around him. But Peter and John demand his attention. He lifts his eyes warily to see these two burly fishermen from the Galilee. I can't help but wonder whether the crippled man at first was as disappointed as I had been standing on that cold door step watching a leaflet with the name "Jesus" float down into my pillowcase. "Silver or gold we have not," the missionary disciple says, "but all that I have I give—in the strong name of Jesus stand and walk."

The power of the Holy Spirit descends upon the man and he rises to his feet overjoyed with his restored health. He clings to Peter and John and enters into the temple rejoicing. The worshipping congregation is shocked as they all recognize the man to whom they have been offering tokens of kindness down through the years at the beautiful gate, likely the double gate on the southern entrance. They gather at Solomon's porch, a spot usually used for Greeks and other Gentiles who traveled to visit the temple. Peter and John are huddled together like a shy bride and groom at their wedding reception trying to decide who would speak first at the microphone. Somebody has to say something. Somebody has to preach. Somebody has to say the Name.[3]

We've all had those moments in our lives where we hesitate to say a name. I recall being asked to say grace one Christmas Day at an unusually quiet extended family gathering. Newcomers to the family, boyfriends and girlfriends, often commented how boisterous and extroverted our family gatherings were—but not this year. We gathered for Christmas dinner just a few months after my cousin Cal was killed in an accident in northern Manitoba, leaving a young wife and two small sons behind. We gathered

3. The need for a witness in a post-Christendom context with the courage to proclaim the name of Jesus is clear. It is important to acknowledge Walter Brueggemann's caution, however, that "naming the name" without acknowledging a larger context is not helpful. Brueggemann reminds us that the Hebrew word *bissar* means "tell the news" and that this message *announced* is critical. Someone has to say the name but that proclamation is in light of God's action and must be followed by transformed action in the world. Brueggemann suggests interpreting evangelism in three scenes: 1) conflict between powerful forces; 2) the witness who gives testimony and tells the outcome (Peter would be an example in the reading from Acts); and 3) the listener then is invited to make an appropriate response. Brueggemann, *Biblical Perspectives on Evangelism*, 15–18.

in grief and remembrance and we gathered to pray. As grace was said I simply acknowledged our deep sense of loss and longing for Cal's presence. Afterwards, as food was shared and wine flowed the atmosphere picked up. My aunt came over to me and quietly said how thankful she was that I had simply said Cal's name . . . how difficult it is sometimes just to say the name.

It was a lesson for me that simply saying the name can bring healing. As Christians we acknowledge that there is ultimately One name, the name above all names—the name Scripture says is the source for every family on earth—the name Scripture says that at the last every knee shall bow. This One name brings healing, wholeness, salvation. Silver or gold I have not but all that I have I give you, in the name of Jesus stand up and walk.

The mainline Protestant church in Canada from the 1950s on tried very hard to be all things to all people. As we've mentioned earlier through Leonard Sweet's writing, it became in many ways what sociologist Roy Olderberg calls "the third place"—the place between work and home that has meaning like *Cheers,* "where everybody knows your name." The church became a place not only for religious ritual but also for social gatherings, sports events, community dinners, and so forth. Taken to the extreme you reach an experience of church that has less and less to do with preaching and living the gospel.

A friend of mine from seminary named Miriam was ordained and her first charge was a collection of five churches in rural Newfoundland. When she arrived and started touring the congregations she discovered the fifth point no longer held regular worship services nor were the people interested in worship—they were using the old church as a beer hall and darts parlor in the village. She resolved with the Session to close the church and the local police officer thought it might be a good idea to escort the young pastor as she went to lock the place up for the last time.

No, the days of an "attraction model through programs" is waning. Silver and gold I have not, but let all that I have in the name of Jesus rise. Soong-Chan Rah notes that after decades of "church growth" modeled on North American business models this

> succeeding generation of churches has begun to recognize that an affluenza and market-driven church that appeals to materialistic desires of the individual consumer has resulted in a comfortable church, but not a biblical church. The church's captivity to materialism has resulted in the unwillingness to confront sins such

as economic and racial injustice and has produced consumers of religion rather than followers of Jesus.[4]

Rah's comments, perhaps an echo of Pierre Burton's infamous 1966 work *The Comfortable Pew*, remind us why missional leadership is critical for Christ's church in North America today and into the future. Not simply that teaching and ruling elders would be able to articulate the faith but that each and every baptized Christian might have the courage to offer a witness, a testimony to the hope that is within you and me. Is it because like poor Peter and John we are simply too intimidated to speak of our faith in public? Many are terrified by the idea of having to describe openly the work of God in our lives or the lives of others. In fact, when something significant happens in our life how do we often respond? Sometimes we play it down with humor or sarcasm. Sometimes we take credit for the mysterious change of events ourselves. Sometimes we give others credit, but rarely do we give God the glory. For most polite, well-mannered, and well-groomed Reformed Christians, we suffer from liturgical laryngitis—in other words, we are tongue-tied Christians.

And yet, there are times in our lives, based on our experience, or you might say in light of God's revelation, that somebody has to say something, somebody needs to preach, somebody needs to say the name, the name of Jesus. I was reminded of reading an essay in Canada's national newspaper *The Globe and Mail,* where a young woman described coming to terms with her younger sister's sudden death around Easter the year before. Although raised in a Christian home she had never understood the real power of Jesus until her sister's death. While some expected her to lose her faith as a result of this death, she described the experience of living into the power of Easter for the first time in her life. More powerful than cards, good wishes, the kindness of employers, or the promise that her sister would live on in memories, the young woman said that for the first time "heaven had a face." As a result healing started to happen. *Silver or gold I have none but all that I have I give you, in the name of Jesus stand and walk.*

There are times and places where we need to speak the name of Jesus. We have to say *the* name. You know, the name above all names. Peter and John were at one of those moments. Somebody had to preach. Somebody had to say something. Somebody had to *say the name*. Peter and John understood that some word of explanation must be offered. People shouldn't be confused or tricked into thinking that this healing was by their own

4. Rah, *Next Evangelicalism*, 63.

hand. Peter and John named the source of their healing in Jesus Christ, the risen one, who once rejected, now must be received so that their sins may be wiped out. Wiped clean like years ago when we were moving across the country and had just finished cleaning and painting our house to go on the market for sale. My wife called in a panic saying that there was a showing in one hour and that I needed to come home and sort out a disaster. I arrived home and discovered that one of our children had taken a blue ballpoint pen and drawn pictures all over the freshly painted white kitchen wall. My daughter stood repentantly in the corner staring at the ground. I looked again at the little stick figure she had drawn with goofy eyes and stringy hair and something changed inside me. God's Spirit moved me from anger to forgiveness to love and even a little bit of humor. I put my arms around her and said, "I love you, I forgive you—now, don't ever do that again!" And then, using this generation's panacea, I found a solution on the Internet using hairspray and a cloth. I watched as the blue ink miraculously disappeared from the wall leaving no mark of the mess behind. It was like an echo of when Scripture says, "Come let us reason together, for your sins are like scarlet and I will make them as white as snow."[5]

With this same confidence that all wrongs could be set right by the grace and power of God in Jesus Christ, that day long ago Peter boldly proclaimed:

> Oh, Israelites, why does this take you by such complete surprise, and why stare at us as if our power or piety made him walk? The God of Abraham and Isaac and Jacob, the God of our ancestors, has glorified his Son Jesus. The very One that Pilate called innocent, you repudiated. You repudiated the Holy One, the Just One, and asked for a murderer in his place. You no sooner killed the Author of Life than God raised him from the dead—and we're the witnesses. Faith in Jesus' name put this man, whose condition you know so well, on his feet—yes, faith and nothing but faith put this man healed and whole right before your eyes. And now, friends, I know you had no idea what you were doing when you killed Jesus, and neither did your leaders. But God, who through the preaching of all the prophets had said all along that his Messiah would be killed, knew exactly what you were doing and used it to fulfill his plans. Now it's time to change your ways! Turn to face God so he

---

5. Isaiah 1:18, *NRSV.*

can wipe away your sins, pour out showers of blessing to refresh
you, and send you the Messiah he prepared for you, namely, Jesus.[6]

Today, missional leadership in a culture of affluence holds the Laodicean
cure right where it has always been—at the heart of the gospel of our risen
Lord Jesus Christ. But somebody has to preach. Somebody has to speak in
an age of post-Christendom when the church's voice is one of many in the
cacophony of this world's values. Somebody has to say something. Somebody has to say the name above all names. Above every corporation and
political party. The name above every lobbyist and special interest group
that holds power. The name above profit and shareholder value. The name
that scolds Laodicea but praises Philadelphia for countercultural faithfulness in a time of great peril. The name that rejects Botox Christianity and
holds fast to the need for the crucified and risen one to bypass our sin. We
know the name.

In the end, we must face the world each and every day in a culture of
affluence that eagerly anticipates the gifts of silver and gold. However, as
children of God, as disciples of Christ, as actors in the Trinity's great story
of salvation, the greatest gift we have is to sit with the beggar's need, to
stand like a child on Halloween with a pillowcase open, to run with joy to
tell others in the shadow of the cross and the brilliant light of the resurrection morn we have been made whole by the strong name of Jesus. It's time
to join God in the neighborhood as missionary disciples. It's time to say the
name. Say the name.

---

6. Acts 3:12–19, *The Message*.

Bibliography

Allen, Ronald. *Preaching and Practical Ministry.* St. Louis: Chalice, 2001.

Baker, Frank. "The Real John Wesley." *Methodist History* 12, July 1974, 183–97.

Barth, Karl. *Evangelical Theology.* Grand Rapids: Eerdmans, 1963.

———. *Final Testimonies.* Eugene, OR: Wipf and Stock, 2013.

Bass, Diana Butler. *Christianity for the Rest of Us: How the Neighborhood Church is Transforming Faith.* San Francisco: Harper Collins, 2006.

Bauckham, Richard. *Bible and Mission: Christian Witness in a Postmodern World.* Grand Rapids: Baker, 2003.

Bell, Rob. *Velvet Elvis: Repainting the Christian Faith.* Grand Rapids: Zondervan, 2005.

Bibby, Reginald. *Restless Churches: How Canada's Churches Can Contribute to the Emerging Religious Renaissance.* Toronto: Novalis, 2004.

Bonhoeffer, Dietrich. *The Cost of Discipleship.* New York: Simon & Schuster, 1959.

———. *Letters and Papers from Prison.* Minneapolis: Fortress, 2009.

Borg, Marcus. *Meeting God Again for the First Time: Beyond Dogmatic Religion to a More Authentic Contemporary Faith.* San Francisco: Harper Collins, 1997.

Bosch, David. "Evangelism: Theological Currents and Cross-Currents Today." In *The Study of Evangelism: Exploring a Mission Practice of the Church,* edited by Paul Chilcote, 4–17. Grand Rapids: Eerdmans, 2008.

———. *Transforming Mission: Paradigm Shifts in Theology of Mission.* Maryknoll, NY: Orbis, 1991.

Bowen, John. *Evangelism for Normal People.* Minneapolis: Fortress, 2002.

Bowen, John, ed. *Green Shoots Out of Dry Ground: Growing a New Future for the Church in Canada.* Eugene, OR: Wipf and Stock, 2013.

Brueggemann, Walter. *Biblical Perspectives on Evangelism: Living in a Three-Storied Universe.* Nashville: Abingdon, 1993.

Busch, Eberhard. *Karl Barth: His Life from Letters and Autobiographical Texts.* London: SCM, 2012.

Calvin, John. *Institutes of the Christian Religion.* Philadelphia: Westminster, 1960.

Carter, Kenneth, Jr. "Recovering Human Nature through Christian Practice for United Methodism." *Quarterly Review* 23, no. 1, Spring 2003, 45–57.

Chilcote, Paul. *The Wesleyan Tradition: A Paradigm for Renewal.* Nashville: Abingdon, 2002.

Chilcote, Paul, ed. *The Study of Evangelism.* Grand Rapids: Eerdmans, 2008.

Bibliography

Collins, Kenneth. *A Real Christian: The Life of John* Wesley. Nashville: Abingdon, 1997.

Davies, Rupert, ed. *The Works of Wesley*. Nashville: Abingdon, 1989.

de Gruchy, Aubin. "Beyond Intention—John Wesley's Intentional and Unintentional Socio-economic Influences on 18th Century England." *Journal of Theology for Southern Africa*, no. 68, September 1989, 75–85.

Duckworth, Jessica. *Wide Welcome: How the Unsettling Presence of Newcomers Can Save the Church*. Minneapolis: Fortress, 2013.

Dunstan, Sylvia. "All who hunger, gather gladly." In *The Book of Praise*, 534. Hudson, Quebec: The Presbyterian Church in Canada, 1997.

Epstein, Joseph. *Envy: The Seven Deadly Sins*. Oxford: Oxford University Press, 2003.

Farris, Stephen. *Preaching that Matters*. Louisville: Westminster/John Knox, 1998.

Florence, Anna Carter. *Preaching as Testimony*. Louisville: Westminster/John Knox, 2007.

Foss, Michael W. *Power Surge: Six Marks of Discipleship for a Changing Church*. Minneapolis: Augsburg Fortress, 2000.

Frost, Michael. *Exiles: Living Missionally in a Post-Christian Culture*. Peabody, MA: Hendrickson, 2006.

———. *The Road to Missional: Journey to the Center of the Church*. Grand Rapids: Baker, 2011.

Green, Christopher. *Doxological Theology: Karl Barth on Divine Providence, Evil and the Angels*. London: T & T Clark, 2011.

Guder, Darrell. *The Continuing Conversion of the Church*. Grand Rapids: Eerdmans, 2000.

Guder, Darrell, ed. *Missional Church: A Vision for the Sending of the Church in North America*. Grand Rapids: Eerdmans, 1998.

Gutierrez, Gustavo. *A Theology of Liberation*. Maryknoll, NY: Orbis, 1988.

Hall, Douglas John. *Why Christian? For Those on the Edge of Faith*. Minneapolis: Fortress, 1998.

Hastings, Ross. *Missional God, Missional Church: Hope for Re-Evangelizing the West*. Downers Grove, IL: InterVarsity, 2012.

Hauerwas, Stanley, and William Willimon. *Resident Aliens: Life in the Christian Colony*. Nashville: Abingdon, 2014.

Heitzenrater, Richard. *Wesley and the People Called Methodists*. Nashville: Abingdon, 1995.

Hirsch, Alan. *The Forgotten Ways*. Grand Rapids: Brazos, 2009.

Hirsch, Alan, and Darryn Altclass. *The Forgotten Ways Handbook: A Practical Guide for Developing Missional Churches*. Grand Rapids: Brazos, 2009.

Honeycutt, Frank. *Preaching for Adult Conversion and Commitment*. Nashville: Abingdon, 2003.

Jelland, Roger, and Leonard Hjalmarson. *Missional Spirituality: Embodying God's Love from the Inside Out*. Downer's Grove, IL: InterVarsity, 2011.

Johnson, Patrick W. T. *The Mission of Preaching: Equipping the Community for Faithful Witness*. Downer's Grove, IL: InterVarsity, 2015.

Kallenberg, Brad. *Live to Tell: Evangelism in a Postmodern Age*. Grand Rapids: Brazos, 2002.

Kent, John. *Wesley and the Wesleyans*. Cambridge: Cambridge University Press, 2002.

Kimball, Dan. *The Emerging Church: Vintage Christianity for New Generations*. Grand Rapids: Zondervan, 2003.

Lewis, C. S. *The Essential C. S. Lewis*. New York: Touchstone, 1988.

———. *Mere Christianity*. London: Harper Collins, 1998.

Bibliography

————. *Mere Christianity.* New York: MacMillan, 1960.

Lim, Isaac. "Wesleyan Preaching and the Small Group Ministry—Principles and Practices." *Asia Journal of Theology* 3, October 1989, 509–23.

Lockhart, Ross. *Gen X, Y Faith? Getting Real with God.* Kelowna, BC: Wood Lake, 2002.

Long, Tom. *Testimony: Talking Ourselves into Being Christian.* San Francisco: Jossey-Bass, 2004

Luther, Martin. *On Christian Liberty.* Minneapolis: Fortress, 2003.

Mark, Robin. *Come Heal This Land.* Liner notes. Eastbourne, UK: Integrity, 2001.

Martin, David. *Pentecostalism: The World Their Parish.* Oxford: Blackwell, 2002.

McNeal, Reggie. *The Future Present: Six Tough Questions for the Church.* San Francisco: Jossey-Bass, 2009.

Migliorie, Daniel. *Faith Seeking Understanding: An Introduction to Christian Theology.* 2nd ed. Grand Rapids: Eerdmans, 2004.

Milburn, Geoffrey, and Margaret Batty. *Workaday Preachers: The Story of Methodist Local Preaching.* Peterborough, UK: Methodist Publishing House, 1995.

Moore, Robert. *John Wesley and Authority: A Psychological Perspective.* Missoula, MT: Scholars, 1979.

Murray, Stuart. *Church Planting: Laying the Foundations.* Waterloo, Ontario: Herald, 2001.

Newbigin, Lesslie. *The Gospel in a Pluralist Society.* Grand Rapids: Eerdmans, 1989

————. *The Open Secret: An Introduction to the Theology of Mission.* Grand Rapids: Eerdmans, 1995.

Outler, Albert C., ed. *John Wesley.* New York: Oxford University Press, 1964.

Outler, Albert C., and Richard P. Heitzenrater, eds. *John Wesley's Sermons: An Anthology.* Nashville: Abingdon, 1991.

Pathak, Jay, and Dave Runyon. *The Art of Neighboring: Building Genuine Relationships Right Outside Your Door.* Grand Rapids: Baker, 2012.

Placher, William. *The Domestication of Transcendence: How Modern Theology Went Wrong.* Louisville: Westminster/John Knox, 1996.

Pope Francis. *Evangelii Gaudium: The Joy of the Gospel.* Washington, DC: United States Conference of Catholic Bishops, 2014.

Rack, Henry. *Reasonable Enthusiast: John Wesley and the Rise of Methodism.* 3rd ed. London: Epworth, 2014.

Rah, Soong-Chang. *The Next Evangelicalism: Freeing the Church from Western Cultural Captivity.* Downer's Grove, IL: InterVarsity, 2009.

Rogal, Samuel "Counting the Congregation: Wishful Thinking Verses Hard Reality in the Journals of John Wesley." *Methodist History* 30, no. 1, October 1991, 233–44.

Rollins, Peter. *How (Not) to Speak of God.* Brewster, MA: Paraclete, 2006.

Roxburgh, Allan J. *Missional: Joining God in the Neighborhood.* Grand Rapids: Baker, 2011.

————. *The Missional Leader: Equipping Your Church to Reach a Changing World.* San Francisco: Jossey-Bass, 2011.

————. *Missional Mapmaking: Skills for Leading in a Time of Transition.* San Francisco: Jossey-Bass, 2009.

Roxburgh, Allan J., and M. Scott Boren. *Introducing the Missional Church: What It Is, Why It Matters, How to Become One.* Grand Rapids: Baker, 2009.

Rack, Henry. *Reasonable Enthusiast: John Wesley and the Rise of Methodism.* 3rd ed. London: Epworth, 2002.

Rollins, Peter. *How (Not) to Speak of God.* Brewster, MA: Paraclete, 2006.

Bibliography

Rouse, Rick, and Craig Van Gelder. *A Field Guide for the Missional Congregation: Embarking on a Journey of Transformation*. Minneapolis: Fortress, 2008.

Sanneh, Lamin. *Translating the Message: The Missionary Impact on Culture*. Maryknoll, NY: Orbis, 2002.

Saunders, Stanley, and Charles Campbell. *The Word on the Street: Performing the Scriptures in the Urban Context*. Grand Rapids: Eerdmans, 2000.

Slaatte, Howard. *A Purview of Wesley's Theology*. Lanham, MD: University Press of America, 2000.

Sparks, Paul, Tim Soerens, and Dwight Friesen, eds. *The New Parish: How Neighborhood Churches are Transforming Mission, Discipleship and Community*. Downers Grove, IL: InterVarsity, 2014.

Stetzler, Ed. *Planting Missional Churches*. London: Broadman and Holman, 2009.

Stacey, John, ed. *John Wesley: Contemporary Perspectives*. London: Epworth, 1988.

Stone, Bryan. *Evangelism after Christendom: The Theology and Practice of Christian Witness*. Grand Rapids: Brazos, 2007.

Sweet, Leonard. *The Gospel According to Starbucks: Living with a Grand Passion*. Colorado Springs: WaterBrook, 2007.

Taylor, Charles. *A Secular Age*. Cambridge: Harvard University Press, 2007.

Thurman, Howard. "The Sound of the Genuine." Baccalaureate Address, Spelman College, May 4, 1980.

Turner, John. *John Wesley: The Evangelical Revival and the Rise of Methodism in England*. London: Epworth, 2002.

Tyson, John. *Charles Wesley: A Reader*. Oxford: Oxford University Press, 1989.

Van Gelder, Craig. *The Ministry of the Missional Church: A Community led by the Spirit*. Grand Rapids: Baker, 2007.

———. *The Missional Church and Leadership Development*. Grand Rapids: Eerdmans, 2009.

Van Gelder, Craig, ed. *The Missional Church and Denominations: Helping Congregations Develop a Missional Identity*. Grand Rapids: Eerdmans, 2008.

Van Gelder, Craig, and Dwight J. Zscheile, eds. *The Missional Church in Perspective: Mapping Trends and Shaping the Conversation*. Grand Rapids: Baker, 2011.

Wakefield, Gordon. *Methodist Spirituality*. Peterborough, UK: Epworth, 1999.

Webber, Robert. *Ancient Future Evangelism: Making Your Church a Faith Forming Community*. Grand Rapids: Baker, 2007.

Wesley, John. *The Journal of John Wesley*. Chicago: Moody, 1951.

Wilson, Jonathan. *God So Loved the World: A Christology for Disciples*. Grand Rapids: Baker, 2001.